REMEMBERING WORLD WAR II

VE Day, Bridport, 1945

In a brief address to the assembled crowds, the Mayor of Bridport, Councillor S.J. Gale said, "Now that German organised resistance has ceased in Europe... every man and woman in this country can take a personal pride in the wonderful victory that has been achieved."

REMEMBERING WORLD WAR II
WEST DORSET AT WAR

Bridport Heritage Forum

Creeds the Printers, Broadoak, Bridport, Dorset DT6 5NL
Tel. 01308 423411

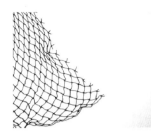

The Bridport Heritage Forum

The Bridport Heritage Forum came together after the success of putting on an exhibition to mark the Queen's Golden Jubilee in 2002, which looked at how Bridport had changed in 50 years.

Made up of interested local groups, the Forum is keen to promote Bridport and the surrounding area, through exhibitions, talks, study days and working with the wider community.

Organisations:

Bridport History Society
West Dorset Research Centre
Bridport Museum
Bridport Camera Club
Bridport Town Council
West Dorset Group, Somerset & Dorset
    Family History Society
Bridport News
Bridport Library
Friends of Bridport Museum
Bridport Arts Centre

Individual members: Jane Ferentzi-Sheppard, Sheila Meaney and Charles Wilde

First published in 2005 as part of the Bridport Heritage Forum's "V for Victory" commemorative events to mark the 60th anniversary of the end of the World War II.

ISBN: 0-9545479-1-8

Compiled, designed and edited by Paul Willis

Printed by Creeds the Printers, Broadoak, Bridport, Dorset, DT6 5NL

Sponsored by Home Front Recall.

Supported by

CONTENTS

Introduction

In 2005 the Bridport Heritage Forum organised a series of events to commemorate the ending of the Second World War. The Forum prepared a variety of activities such as a 1940s Dance, an exhibition of a 1940s house, a children's party, and a veteran's memorial service. This booklet is composed of papers from local historians who have a strong interest in the Second World War. Some of the authors lived in West Dorset during the War, while others are 'incomers' who have relocated to the area after this time. Most importantly, the papers cover a variety of themes which brings this unique period of West Dorset's history to life.

The Second World War was the defining moment of the 20th Century. The War was a time of great upheaval and uncertainty, with many men enlisting to fight overseas; large numbers of women working for Victory in such areas as farm labouring, and factory production; and train-loads of children evacuated from their homes to the relative safety of countryside. In addition, people had to cope with the air raids, blackouts, rationing of items (and the subsequent queues), and the *Make Do and Mend* approach to winning the War. The hardships were universal in unifying the British people towards the War effort. This in itself created a culture of solidarity that permeated the British psyche during the War. Throughout the country, in every city, town and village, the people of Britain encountered the same fears, restrictions, misfortunes and grievances together, in order to create a better world for the future.

Michael Corgan's paper provides an insight into the life of Bridport during the Second World War. Although the town may not have experienced the hardships of some of her neighbouring towns or cities, such as Weymouth, Poole or Southampton, it did feel an important duty to work together in fundraising and housing evacuees for the War effort.

West Dorset was not exempt from the ferocity of the War. On a number of occasions, the War actually reared itself overhead. Many people in Bridport witnessed the dogfights that were synonymous with the Battle of Britain. After attacking other parts of the country, Nazi bombers would frequently jettison any remaining bombs over West Dorset. Valerie Jeanes' paper outlines the destruction and impact of two bombing raids on Bridport during 1942. The indiscriminate nature of the War is brought to life with Mr Creek's daughter's recollection of returning home from a picnic to hear the news that her father had been killed during a bombing raid on Bridport.

Many children who grew up during the years 1939-1945 could not remember a life without the War. The necessity of carrying a gasmask to school, becoming accustomed to the air raid bell and knowing what to do, and seeing family and friends leave to serve overseas, were all part of the life of a child growing up in West Dorset. Janet Boon-Tilley in her paper informs us that she did not think anything odd about the changes brought about by the War, such as the air raid sirens, dogfights overhead, her father going to work on an uncle's farm, and the servicemen everywhere. She accepted it as normality. Although they grew up without the luxuries of future generations, the children of the War years found their pleasures from the simple things of life. Elizabeth Gale (nee Buckler) grew up in Burton Bradstock during the War and mentions the joy of sharing almonds with a soldier who had returned from Italy. Like most children at the time, she was aware of her parents' fear of the War and its ultimate consequences. Elizabeth recollects that her parents did not hide any of the realities of the War from her. Both papers recollect the excitement and changes that the American soldiers brought to Dorchester and Burton Bradstock during this period.

The papers from Fiona Taplin and Sheila Meaney are informative on how the schools in Bridport were affected by the War. The schools in Bridport were stretched to capacity due to the number of evacuees that arrived in Bridport shortly after the start of the Second World War. As the class sizes were becoming unmanageable, local children were to be taught in the mornings, while evacuee children had their lessons in the afternoon. Both papers offer an insight into the ingenuity of the teachers in coping with large class sizes, air raids (including bomb damage), losing teachers to military service, limited budgets, and fund-raising campaigns.

The Second World War affected people on the Home Front in many differing ways. The threat of air raids, food shortages, streets blackened, and of course, being separated from family and friends overseas. In West Dorset, and across the country, people worked long hours for the war effort. The government was concerned that disillusionment on the Home Front could lead to unrest and eventually lead to defeat, and for this reason censorship and propaganda were used to maintain morale. Holly Robinson's paper details the purpose of the *Bridport News* as a vehicle for disseminating War-time information and propaganda. Although local papers such as the *Bridport News* were restricted on what they could and could not report, they helped to promote the notion that with a concerted effort Britain could win the War. War-time slogans such as "Your garden versus U-boats" featured in many local papers at the time.

The Second World War produced literally thousands of heroic individuals who are known through their bravery and their acts of courage under extreme conditions. Rene Gerryts paper brings to light the courage and dedication of one man from West Dorset, Bill Budden. Bill Budden trained as a navigator in the early phases of the War. He was heavily involved with parachute drops and towing gliders on D-Day. After the Allied advances in Europe, Bill continued re-supplying the army with medical equipment, ammunition, and fuel. Near the end of the War he even brought back Prisoners of War and those who had survived the Nazi concentration camps.

The WLA (Women's Land Army) sometimes referred as the "Forgotten Army" was originally established in 1917 as food production had dwindled during the Great

War. In June 1939, the WLA was re-established initially asking for volunteers and later by conscription with numbers reaching approximately 80,000 by 1944. Robin Pearce outlines the role and conditions of the young women who joined the Land Army and who worked in Beaminster during the War. Young women from all across the country arrived in Beaminster to work as part of the Land Army. They worked long, hard gruelling hours. Homesickness was also a major problem as many had not been away from their family for long periods before. It has been recorded that this was particularly true for the many women who were billeted to farms. While others, like the Land Army Girls in Beaminster who stayed in the local hostel, were happier as they were grouped together and a genuine feeling of camaraderie developed.

It is only through the stories of those who lived and survived the days of the Second World War that we can ever try to understand what it was like. Although we can never really know, it is only through their stories of survival, determination and courage that we can ever hope to do so. Jane Ferentzi-Sheppard provides four individual stories of people managing to cope with the changes that the War had caused to their lives.

After the fall of France and with the threat of invasion looming overhead, the government created a force of civilian volunteers (Auxiliary Units), recruited mainly from the Home Guard, who were to operate from secret underground bases and sabotage the supply lines of the invading German army. Bob Pearson relates the experiences of George Raymond, the only surviving member of a six-man Auxiliary Unit based in Beaminster. George was trained in sabotage techniques and became especially adept in the use of explosives. The Auxiliary Units were not expected to operate for a long period; the chances of them surviving were at the most a few weeks. Considering the task facing them, Bob Pearson's paper shows a brave man's humour and dedication to a task for which he was willing to die, which was indicative of many people during the War.

The Dieppe Raid on occupied France on August 19, 1942 was an ill-fated disaster. Sheila Meaney's in-depth account of the Yukon Exercises informs us there is no such thing as a fool-proof military operation. The first Yukon Exercise undertaken off the West Dorset coast near Bridport was a 'dismal failure'. While the second was more successful, this success did not eventuate on the Dieppe Raid. Although Lord Louis Mountbatten, head of Combined Operations during World War Two, received much criticism because of the high casualty rate of the Raid, he commented "For every man who died in Dieppe at least ten or more must have been spared in Normandy in 1944."

By the end of January 1944 almost a million American GIs are crammed into southern England. The number of American GIs in Dorset was approximately 80000. The 'invasion' of so many Americans became a cultural exchange whereby American cigarettes, chewing gum, chocolate bars, nylon stockings, music, and slang was reciprocated with pipe smoking, real ales and ciders, Britain's rich and diverse history, tea and traditional British food. The popularity of the Americans, with their abundant wealth of assorted goods was admired by most of the population. However this caused some to characterise the GIs as "Overpaid, Oversexed, and Over Here." Robin Pearce's paper brings to life the American 'invasion' of Bridport. It was an exciting time for the inhabitants of Bridport. Pearce suggests that one in every three people in Bridport at this time was an American soldier. Chris Pamplin's paper concentrates on Sergeant Raymond Mohrlang who was stationed in Bridport during the build up to D-Day. It is poignant to view the photographs of Raymond Mohrlang and his comrades who were preparing to fight across Europe for freedom. As Gary Mohrlang (Raymond Mohrlang's son) relates, friendships and memories were established during the War that time could never erase.

The friendly, and in some cases, life changing interactions between the Americans and the local people of West Dorset has become folk-lore. Many stories exist of how the GIs handed out food items and equipment to the rationed locals; and how the locals welcomed the Americans into their homes with grace and humour. Celia Martin, provides two stories of how two Americans that were stationed in Bridport during the War, and how it had a lasting effect on lives. Overall, the stories bring to life, the everlasting relationships that were established during the War. Joseph Parke, a Private with the 16th Infantry of the First United States Army met and married Mary Conlon in Bridport in 1944. Muriel Engelman was billeted at Downe Hall, Bridport for a month during 1944. She made friends with Mr and Mrs S. R. Edwards, who lived on West Bay Road. After over sixty years she has recently made contact with the Edwards' grandchildren.

Nigel Clarke's paper highlights the American GI presence in Lyme Regis during the Second World War. In particular the paper brings to light the inequality between the black and white GIs and the unofficial segregation that permeated the American presence in Britain during the War. In 1942, on the eve of the 'friendly invasion' by the GIs, the British Government passed the *Visiting Forces Act* which gave the American military the right to use capital punishment as an extension of discipline. The main purpose of capital punishment was a means of controlling: a) the perceived danger of Black GIs socialising with British females; and b) the possible violence between Black and White American soldiers. Nigel Clarke's paper details the tensions between the two groups that escalated into violence in late May 1944.

The Black Panther Division, the 66th Infantry Division arrived in England, 26 November 1944. By 12 December 1944, the Division had approximately 5,500 personnel in West Dorset. Jane Ferentzi-Sheppard recalls the harrowing story of the Division's fatal journey from England to France on 24 December 1944. The paper highlights how chance and fate can have such enormous consequences. The War was an indiscriminate killer of lives. Many attest that it was purely good fortune that they survived the War.

"This is your victory," Churchill cried from the balcony of Whitehall on 8th May 1945. "Everyone, man or woman, has done their best." Although, this did not officially mark the end of the War, (VJ Day was still three months away) Churchill's statement addresses the fact that the Second World War was the People's War. The end of the War brought a sense that Britain and the world would be a better place. Britain could look forward to the emergence of the welfare state. However the immediate post-war years were materially harsher than the years during the War. Rationing remained and grew stricter. The country was bankrupt, surviving only on an American loan. Paul Willis comments on the aftermath of the War focusing particularly on Bridport during the years 1945-1953. Bridport suffered the restrictions and rationing after the War like other towns across the country. Life was also changing at a dramatic rate with new industries developing and others opening up new markets across the world. During this time, Bridport's main industry, rope and net-making, was under threat from new competition overseas and the introduction of synthetic fibres. By mid 1953, Bridport was looking to the future by revisiting its industrious past in commemorating the Charter of 1253, which celebrated the ingenuity, creativity and uniqueness of the town.

Before the War, West Dorset was an area somewhat removed from the troubles and strifes of the outside world. It was a place where families, friends and communities lived side by side for generations. The Second World War heralded a time of change. The War touched the lives of everyone in West Dorset in one way or another. The collection of papers contained in this publication provides an insight into those times and how the courage of the people of West Dorset and visitors to area, coped in a situation that was at the time the most destructive the world had ever witnessed.

Paul Willis
June 2005

Bridport at War (1939-1945)

by Michael Corgan

As everywhere else in the U.K. evacuation, conscription, shortages and rationing, and enemy action had their effects on the small community of Bridport, though not to the same extent as in the big cities, but nevertheless keenly felt.

September 2nd 1939

1400 evacuees arrived from Paddington, then a poor part of London. The condition of many of the slum children opened the eyes of the people of Bridport. The town rose to meet their needs, and though some Londoners found the quiet and slow pace hard to bear, many settled happily and a few are still here!

C (Bridport) Company Home Guard 1944
© Photograph courtesy of the Bridport Museum Trust

War work in the town and on the land

Meanwhile many of the men folk were called up. For those left behind War meant long hours at work and long evenings in Civil Defence occupations. As well as Air Raid Wardens, the Auxiliary Fire Service and later, compulsory fire-watching, many served in the Observer Corps, the Home Guard and a select few in a little known arm of the Home Guard – the Auxiliary Units. Four of these had hidden bases in the countryside around Bridport. Their role was to disrupt German communications and morale in the event of an invasion. They were part of the world's first official resistance movement set up in advance of an invasion. At the same time the women of Bridport rallied to the WVS, (Womens Voluntary Service) providing an amazingly comprehensive service looking after the welfare of the civilian population as well as that of the troops, both those posted here in Bridport, and those away from home. All in all some half of the pre-war population were involved in these activities.

Meanwhile the traditional netting industry went into overdrive, producing vast quantities of nets – camouflage, both large for vehicles and planes, small for tin helmets, and scrambling nets for landing and naval craft. Millions of pullthroughs, for cleaning rifles, were made by outworkers – the going rate was 5 shillings (25p) a hundred! Other war work included the highly secret plant, set up in a memorial mason's works, making a vital part of the sonar submarine detection gear used in the Battle of the Atlantic and in many other seas around the world. Aircraft parts were made at the Brit Engineering Works, where employees worked twelve hour shifts, six and seven day weeks to get vitally needed supplies to the forces. While these heavy commitments were being undertaken in the town, the surrounding countryside was also undergoing vast changes. A huge increase in the acreage cultivated was made, with much help from the Government using local people to oversee and implement initiatives to safeguard Britain from being starved into submission. An extra 6000 acres of land was to be put into production in this area. With so many younger men in the Forces the Women's Land Army brought city girls to the farm, where they worked hard alongside the initially doubting men.

Enemy action

In 1942 two air raids took place, both from hit and run planes coming in off the sea. Seven people died in these raids, and there were some 20 houses destroyed and many more suffered damage. Fortunately these proved to be isolated incidents – there was no further bombing – but the raids are remembered vividly to this day. Many people saw the bombs dropping, and of course in so small a community many knew the casualties well. One of the eyewitnesses was in his late teens and recalled a raid: "I'd been sent down to town by my mother to do some shopping ...... I was there when the plane came, and the bomb was dropped.... I was in the A.T.C. and I knew the plane, so I dived under the seat outside the old Post Office. And I saw two people killed." There were two other minor actions nearby – a raid on the village of Chideock, where damage was slight, and a machine-gun attack on a coastal artillery site at West Bay. But fortunately no casualties were recorded in these incidents.

New faces, new habits

As well as the evacuees other new faces and accents came to Bridport during the six years of the war. British regiments were here from across the UK: West Kents, Essex, South Lancashire, the Cameronians complete with pipe band, and the Royal Welsh Fusiliers, no pipes, but a big billy goat as mascot, and then the Canadians, practising for the disastrous raid on Dieppe, landed at West Bay. But far and away the biggest influx in every sense was that of the US 16th Infantry Regiment stationed here in the 7-month run up to D-Day. Arriving at a time when the hardships of war were really biting, the generosity of all things American, especially the men with their food rations, was a huge contrast to the lean time that Bridport was experiencing, in common with the rest of Britain. Many friendships were formed before the US troops left for Normandy, and some friends still visit each other today.

There were two famous visitors during the course of the war. Because of security needs no fuss was made. King George VI came to Bridport to review troops in the area. And General Montgomery was here

King George VI leaving the Bull Hotel, Bridport, Sept 1939.
© Photograph courtesy of the Bridport Museum Trust

too, firstly as GOC Southern Command to watch rehearsals for the Dieppe raid (and was less than impressed by the first one) and then in connection with the forthcoming invasion of Europe.

What was it like here during the War?

There were shortages of everything! Food was, of course, rationed. Unrationed items were scarce and at the rumour of new deliveries queues formed with lightning speed. Fuel too was rationed, usually only one room could be kept heated. Nights were pitch black, a blackness enforced rigorously by Air Raid Wardens ensuring that no chink of light would attract enemy bombers. But there was much social activity in the town, involving both the town people and the troops. Two cinemas and regular dances kept the young folk entertained, and although visits to the beaches were not permitted there was still plenty of countryside for walking. And much walking was done as transport also suffered from fuel rationing. Little fuel was available for private cars but trains still served Bridport and it was possible to get about. Despite, or because of the restrictions, shortages and genuine hardship, a feeling of community involvement grew here. For its size Bridport made astounding contributions to the Home Guard and voluntary services, where something in the order of 60% of the population were involved in one role or another; to the National Savings movement, under which enormous sums were raised – for example a *War Weapons Week* in 1941 had a target of £45,000 but raised an incredible £201,000. In May 1941 *Wings for Victory Week* raised nearly £6000, which was used to buy a Spitfire, named "The Brit". In 1942 *Warship Week* was opened by the distinguished Admiral, Reginald Plunkett-Ernle-Erle-Drax, with a target of £70,000. The sum raised was £169,117 and the people of Bridport were told it had purchased a minesweeper named after the town.

Multiply that by 40 to get an idea of what that means in today's' values! Consider too that the majority of the population were working people, and they were not very well paid either. Another area of saving was that of salvage – everything that could be used for the war effort was contributed by the local people; iron railings from their front gardens, waste paper, and aluminium in huge quantities, mainly saucepans old and new.

Returning servicemen remarked on how tired the town looked by the end of the war. There had been neither paint nor building materials spare for maintenance and renovation. In addition, it was noticed how tired the people were who had worked so hard during the period of hostilities, supporting the fighting men and living on basics, with little time to relax or luxuries to enjoy. It had in all ways been a hard war, and there was much rejoicing when victory was finally won.

"The Brit" spitfire financed through donations collected from the Bridport area during the 'Wings for Victory Week', May 1941.
© Photograph courtesy of the Bridport Museum Trust

Bombing at Bridport

by Valerie Jeanes

This article is based on interviews taken about twenty years ago with some additional information I have received recently.

War with Germany was expected long before 1939 and in September 1938 Bridport Borough Council announced a scheme for the evacuation of the population to the woods and lanes in the event of an air raid. Details were given to ARP (Air Raid Precaution) wardens to implement these if and when the time came. In July 1939 plans were made for trenches for Allington School and Gundry Lane School (St Mary's Primary School) to be dug in Skilling. The boys at the Grammar School in St Andrew's Road dug trenches on the edge of their field. Neither of these options would have been much use. The Grammar School trenches were halfway up Coneygar and although the pupils did go up there wearing old coats in a suitable colour for camouflage, after a few months it was decided this wasted too much time and the pupils stayed at their desks, ready to dive under them if necessary. It is difficult to imagine children from North Allington and Gundry Lane being marshalled to Skilling.

In June 1940 Dorset County Council gave permission for six cellars in the town to be used as shelters and the Borough Council agreed to strengthen six others at a cost of £400. There was one beneath what is now Browns the Opticians and another in East Street.

After the fall of France in June 1940 the south coast was easily accessible to German planes. Between August 1940 to October 1941 the Bridport area had 1145 yellow air raid warnings and 283 red ones. After October 1941 yellow warnings were not recorded. Most of these were associated with bombing raids aiming for Yeovil, Bristol, the Midlands, Weymouth or Portland, and the local people eventually became used to seeing German planes flying over the town and took little notice of them. I remember my brother and I watching some planes from our garden gate in Orchard Crescent when our mother rushed out and dragged us indoors saying they were Germans.

Numerous 'incidents' as they were called were reported in and around Bridport, mercifully many bombs falling in open fields possibly because they were jettisoned by crews who were under attack not wanting to have live bombs on board.

It became apparent that the arrangements to evacuate were not practicable due to the lack of warning time and because the planes often machine gunned the area. People were now advised to stay in their own homes; under the stairs being the preferred option. I remember we children used to be put under the dining table. Some families had shelters, either outside Anderson ones or indoor Morrison ones which took up much of the living space in a small living room.

On Bank Holiday 2nd August 1942 two fighter bombers came in low from the sea and dropped two bombs on the town before the sirens sounded. Many people were at West Bay and saw them coming in. The first bomb fell in West Street behind what was then the Star Hotel and is now the Dairymaid, killing four people, severely injuring three and slightly injuring twenty-one. All the windows from Bests in West Street to the cinema in South Street were broken. After dropping its bombs the plane flew out over Court Orchard and then returned, machine-gunning the town hitting the town clock, which didn't stop.

Bomb damage, West Street, Bridport, August 1942
© Photograph courtesy of the Bridport Museum Trust

Three of those killed were local people: George Hecks, the son of the licensee of the Star Hotel, who was home on leave, a Mrs Bowerman and a Mrs Cast. Mrs Cast had come to town to post a letter and some say she was killed pushing a child out of the way. The fourth person's identity was a mystery to me for a long time. I knew his name was Mr William Creek because it is on the War Memorial but no-one remembered him. Eventually I advertised in the Bridport News and received a reply from a Mr Stebbings in Beaminster, who told me Mr Creek and his family had come to Bridport to get away from the bombing in Exeter. He also put me in touch with Mr Creek's daughter. I subsequently had a letter from her in which she describes what she remembers of that day.

> My mother, father, two younger sisters and I went to Bridport for a holiday the day before the bomb fell. I was then aged sixteen. The rest of the family were staying with my aunt and uncle (my mother's sister), Mr and Mrs Arthur Bullock who lived in a flat over a menswear shop next door to the Star Hotel. I was staying with another aunt and uncle, Mr and Mrs B Cornick in Victoria Grove, and an aunt who lived with them.
>
> On Sunday 2nd August my two aunts, uncle and I had gone for a day's picnic to a field at Bradpole, where they had a small caravan. In the afternoon, we heard a loud explosion, and saw thick smoke rising over the centre of Bridport, and we were seriously alarmed. My young aunt and I set off across the fields at once, to discover what had happened. On the way, we noticed paper bags, with the name of the outfitters on them, blowing about, and our worst fears were realised. We hurried on to Victoria Grove. The Police were there at the house, and we were told that my father had been killed, and the rest of the household, although bruised, shaken and shocked, were not seriously injured, apart from my youngest sister, aged six, whose thigh was broken.

One of those injured was also on holiday and I recorded his memories on tape. After the bombing he stayed on in Bridport and lived here for the rest of his life. He says:

> It isn't a thing you forget in a hurry. We just came down to Bridport for the weekend....We were living at Ilminster at the time (Mrs Hopkins interjects – we were married a year) and I wanted a week's holiday but the boss said they were too busy. So I said if I can't have a week I'm going to have a weekend.
>
> We came down here for the weekend and got caught in the bombing and have never been back since. We went for a walk on the Sunday at twenty past six. We got just as far as the barbers shop (at the corner of North Street – what is now Jag Communications) and I saw two planes going over the town hall and I said for goodness sake run in that doorway – that's Jerries. We ran for the doorway (of the barbers shop) and at the same time the bomb went off in the back of the Star Hotel and the blast came right through the archway and blew the bottom of the stone bay window right in (of the barbers shop). Another yard and it would have taken our legs right off. We got in the doorway but my left leg wasn't quite clear of the window. Anyway it's funny what blast will do, there was one woman, the landlady, it blew her right up the chimney and when they looked for her they couldn't find her. They just saw her legs dangling. Her son was in the archway and he was killed.

He and the other people who were injured were taken to Christchurch hospital. Mr Hopkins was in hospital for seven months.

The second bomb fell in Rax Lane behind two large stores one of which was called Elmes, a large haberdashery shop which had a glass arcade in the front. Mr Spencer, the owner of Elmes, told me that there were no buildings at the rear of the other store (International Stores) but his premises took the blast. The outside toilets and an old stable were severely damaged. All the glass in Elmes' frontage was blown out.

The congregation of the Unitarian Chapel (the Chapel in the Garden) were at service and a piece of shrapnel fell through one of the windows and damaged one of the pews. They have kept this damage and a plaque records the event.

Bomb damage, Rax Lane, Bridport, August 1942
© Photograph courtesy of the Bridport Museum Trust

On 16th December 1942 at lunch time on a dull day with thick cloud a bomber circled the town on its way (apparently to Portland) and when the guns opened fire it dropped its four bombs on the town. One lodged in the doorway of the Westminster Bank and did not go off, one bombed the square of cottages behind Mr Jowett's Antique Shop in East Street, where the entrance to the car park is now, one dropped on 92-96 East Street, killing Mrs Trevett, Mrs Norman and 3 year old Maureen Ann Wilcox. The fourth dropped on the north side of the road in the field opposite the Masonic Hall making a large hole.

Mr Spencer (Elmes was on the other side of the road opposite the Bank) told me that the road was closed for three days until a bomb disposal team drew the bomb out of the Bank after making it safe and I have recently received a letter from Mr Simmonds who was one of the bomb disposal men together with a photograph of his squad with the bomb. As Elmes still had no windows from the August raid that shop was used as a safety barrier, with the men working a long rope behind Elmes' double doors to draw the bomb onto the pavement outside the Bank and it was then loaded on a lorry and taken away.

The playground of the General School was littered with glass but Miss Fooks, a teacher there, said they were lucky because the blast went the other way towards Bedford Terrace.

Mrs Jean Pomeroy whose family lived in one of three cottages off King Street was bombed out. She doesn't think she heard the bomb drop, just everything collapsing round them. She was never able to go back to the house to collect anything, however she believes looters took away some items as the bomb didn't remove the stair carpet did it? The family were given £70 in compensation. Mr Peter Chick tells me that he came home from school to find debris all over his bed and he still has a piece of shrapnel (a piece of a bomb).

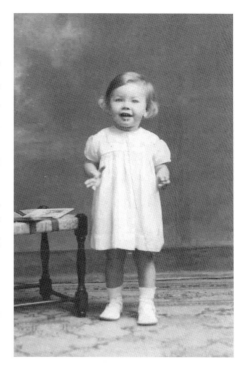

Maureen Ann Willcox was the daughter of Mr and Mrs Bill Willcox.
They lived at Linton Cheney.
While Mr Willcox was serving in the Far East, Maureen and her mother stayed in Bridport with Mrs Willcox's mother. When the bomb went off Maureen was killed and Mrs Willcox was injured.
© Private Collection

Mrs Brenda Dunn, who was just 5 at the time, the grand-daughter of Mrs Trevett, wrote me a letter describing her memories of that day.

The day my Grandmother was killed by a German bomb is etched clearly on my mind for ever.

Gran's name was Emily Jane Trevett, a widow, the mother of 5 girls, and she lived in a cottage at the bottom of East Street, where the long gardens back onto 'back rivers'.

The siren wailed when we were having our dinner. I can't remember ever feeling frightened when the siren sounded, as nothing seemed to happen, except perhaps the distant drone of a plane.

When the 'all clear' sounded we all three went upstairs to see if there had been any damage. My mother went into our little back bedroom that overlooked the river and fields. The fields were used by a local dairy farmer, a Mr Allen, who had some animals and a cowshed in the field directly behind our house. My father and I went into the front bedroom and looked out of the window that faced the Crock Lane turning.

From the back bedroom I heard my mother say: 'The top of Allen's cowshed is gone'. Then a scream, as she turned obviously to look towards the town, 'Oh Mother'.

The smoke and dust my mother could see from that window was the remains of what was her mother's house, now just a pile of rubble. My grandmother was killed instantly, as were other occupants of the neighbouring two or three houses. My father was given compassionate leave to assist the family and joined his unit at a later date, but sadly he too didn't survive the war and died in Normandy.

Emily Jane Trevett. Died at 93 East Street, Bridport, 16 December 1942 by enemy action.
© Private Collection

A Child's Memories of 1939-1945

by Elizabeth Gale

They danced the "Four handed Reel" in the street, to the accompaniment of an accordion. My parents joined in and we youngsters skipped around the periphery, too young to understand the emotional and mental relief that they were feeling. It was May 8th 1945 and the end of the war in Europe. The church bells were ringing. Later, at a celebration party, I was dressed up as Britannia, complete with shield and trident, long white frock made from parachute material and wearing Bridport Fire Chief, Sam Gluning's, brass helmet.

Elizabeth Gale (née Buckler)
aged 5 in 1939
© Private Collection

Nearly six years, before, I had sat with my mother, that Sunday morning and heard the words, "We are at war with Germany". From then on, the wireless was never switched off and I recall waking up in the night, hearing snatches of the news from the World Service and the test tune, "Here Comes the Bogeyman". For us the bogeyman was Hitler. I started school, for the first time, the week that war was declared.

My parents kept nothing from me and as a consequence, I have vivid memories of wartime. My mother's young cousin was killed when the reconnaissance aircraft, on which he was a photographer, was shot down. Two uncles were serving in the forces. The one in the Royal Navy sent us a photograph of a ship iced up. It was apparent from this that he was on the Russian Convoys. He was 'blown up' twice, putting his survival down to swimming all his life, off West Bay, in the cold sea.

The other uncle was in the Royal Air Force in the Far East, for the duration and a third uncle was in "hush-hush" technical work. My favourite aunt was twice bombed out of her home, in London, whilst working as a sister at Guy's Hospital. Later she was seconded, to the army. I admired her smart uniform. Dad was in the Special Constabulary, (I still have his whistle) and my parents befriended many servicemen. All this is plainly etched on my mind.

In the autumn of 1939, evacuees came from London. We had our lessons in the mornings and they used our classroom in the afternoons, when we went out on Nature Walks. We carried our gasmasks in cardboard boxes, rather like the Three Little Foxes, in A.A. Milne's poem carried their handkerchiefs. The windows of the school were gummed over with criss-cross tape, in case there was an air raid and our astute Headmaster, who was a leading light in the ARP, (Air Raid Precaution) did surprise drills. We had to put on our gasmasks and get under the desks. At six years old, this worried me, as I wondered if my parents knew that there was an air-raid. I can't remember being told that it was only pretend.

Elizabeth Gale (née Buckler), seated back row, far left.
An American GI officer visiting Burton Bradstock School in early 1944.
Headmaster R. B. Howarth can be seen standing under the windows.
© Photograph by courtesy of the Imperial War Museum, London

In the country we never went hungry. There were plenty of rabbits and vegetables. Wasn't the slogan, "Dig For Victory", anyway? At school we drank fresh milk and were given Horlicks tablets and rose-hip syrup to supplement our diet. Everyone in the village appeared to dabble in a bit of black market and there were huge tins of dry, army biscuits and condensed milk. Eggs had to be sent to collecting stations, so, even on a farm, we often ate reconstituted egg powder. I remember queuing at the butcher's shop for our meat rations. Practically every other food commodity, clothing, petrol and coal, were rationed. Sweets were few and far between. We had ration books and identity cards and wore identity bracelets, (in case we were killed).

There was a commotion late one wet and windy night, when two soldiers knocked at the door. They were lost, cold and soaked to the skin. My parents took them in, gave them a bed, sending them on their way, at dawn, back to their camp, near Loders. Two aloof households had turned them away and I recall my father speaking very angrily about that. A son, on active service, was killed from each of those homes, shortly afterwards.

There were many nights when we heard enemy aircraft droning overhead. They flew over Burton Bradstock, having crossed the channel en route to bomb Bristol, Bath and Yeovil. They sometimes jettisoned surplus bombs on their return. Most landed in the sea but some fell in the fields nearby. One bomb was only two hundred yards from where we lived. It went straight down into a wet area and only one of our windows was broken by the blast. My father would carry me outside, at night, to witness the guns being fired at sea and around Portland. I can picture incendiary bombs falling, the searchlights everywhere and the sight of barrage balloons, in the sky.

The wireless brought encouragement from Prime Minister Churchill and tips to assist the war effort from the Radio Doctor and Food Minister. I remember hearing Lord Haw Haw broadcasting his propaganda. We all knew that "Careless talk costs lives". We collected waste paper at school, going around to the houses once a week. For this we wore round red, lapel badges. We were 'cogs in the wheel'. When the boys played at being soldiers, we girls had to be the Red Cross nurses. During 'War Weapons Weeks' we sang patriotic songs outside Bridport Town Hall.

The news of young men from Burton Bradstock being killed sticks in my memory. A soldier from Burton Bradstock called and told of his narrow escape from Dunkirk. He recounted how he was fired on as they pulled him into the boat.

The Chesil Beach and hinterland were out of bounds, covered in barbed wire and mines. There were tank traps and pillboxes everywhere. One night the, (usually silent), church bells rang. This was a sign of an invasion. It turned out to be a false alarm but the village men stayed on watch for ages. My father told me that if there was an invasion, all the women and children were to be taken to Beaminster Tunnel, for safety. I doubted that they could transport us the long way there and whether in time.

Aged six, in 1940, I was staying the weekend in Yeovil with family friends. A real adventure it was, too, as Yeovil was bombed and we were woken up in the middle of the night and had to clamber into the Morrison shelter, (a reinforced steel table), in the sitting room. In 1942, I saw hundreds of Canadian troops in our fields on a practice raid for Dieppe. Another year, my parents gave hospitality to a tired British soldier, returned from fighting in Italy. He brought almonds that he had picked off the trees.

The American soldiers arrived in 1943. They were stationed throughout Dorset. My parents befriended many of them. They came for Christmas dinner and enjoyed glasses of local cider with us. One was nicknamed 'Long Bill'. I did not know their surnames, although my mother wrote to some of their families. My father's smoking seemed boosted with Camel cigarettes and we didn't go short of canned fruit.

In June 1944, all the GIs suddenly left the area. I was told that they were going to fight the enemy, in France. We were all sad and worried for them and listened avidly to the news on the wireless. Throughout the night of June 5th/6th 1944, the planes, some with gliders, flew on and on overhead. The fighting on the beaches was bloody but the newspapers never told us the full story.

The day the soldiers received their leaving orders, I was at school but they sneaked out to say "Goodbye" to my parents and left me a black puppy, with the excuse that it was too small for them to take. I called her Normandy, although she was always known as "Little Pupper". She lived to be fifteen.

Several weeks after D-Day, Long Bill came back. I can see him now, walking down the path. A once tall, fine young man, now sad and dejected. He had been wounded. He told us that they had 'lived in their tank for seven weeks'. He was being sent back to the front line again. That was the last we heard of him.

Our Americans found themselves on Omaha Beach, in France. Over the intervening years, I have read and reread all about the Battle of Normandy and how they fought alongside our brave troops and other allies. The cemeteries in France are a harrowing reminder of the sacrifice that thousands of them made.

The black American soldiers followed them into the camps and my parents readily took them in, too. They came to my tenth birthday party, in July 1944, bringing a huge box of fruit candies. We ran races and Corporal Ginlack, an athletic, tall young man, ran against me, letting me win. On behalf of the soldiers, he had composed a poem for my birthday, typed it up and put it in a decorated card that he had made. It is a treasured possession.

Fifty years later, in 1994, an elderly American called at Burton Bradstock Post Office, enquiring for my parents, (long dead by then) and me. No one took his name. I hope it was Long Bill.

A poem for Elizabeth's 10th birthday from the U.S. soldiers
© Private Collection

My Recollections of the War Years in Dorchester

by Janet M. Boon-Tilley

In 1939, I was only five years old, so early memories of the War are hazy, but I do recall that I did not find it unusual having an air raid shelter in the garden, black-out at the windows, a dark blue light bulb in my bedroom, car headlights with metal covers with only a slit for the light to shine through, front garden walls with their railings cut off, streets without gas lamps after dark, servicemen everywhere, though I did wonder why two schoolteachers and two teenage pupils from the Haberdashers school in London lived with us for a while.

I accepted air raid sirens, dog fights overhead either by day or illuminated by searchlights at night, my father suddenly going to work on my uncle's farm and still trying to run his business, as well as going out overnight as an A.R.P. (Air Raid Precaution) warden, and visits from a previously unknown Canadian relative in the Carlton York Regiment.

My 6d. a week pocket money bought a National Savings Stamp, which when I had 15/- worth, was exchanged for certificate which in seven years became £1. What riches!

Janet Boon-Tilley in front of air raid shelter in Dorchester, 1943
© Private Collection

Later, the most memorable event was the day the American convoys arrived in the local tree lined roads. Previously I had known there were Americans camped in Came Woods, and many other wooded areas where they could not be clearly seen from the air, living in Nissen huts, and quite large communities, but prior to D-Day, many more came to the area, and our avenues were ideal places to camouflage the vehicles.

What excitement as the first convoy entered our road, there were Jeeps, tanks, lorries, and armoured vehicles, the occupants of which were throwing sweets and gum to any watching children they saw. After school they were lined up under the trees ready to hand out more goodies, and to talk to us, so we made lots of new friends, but were sad sometimes to find the previous days' men had moved out overnight and a new crowd had moved in.

We children were forbidden by our parents to enter any of the vehicles, and we being innocent could not understand why, but for once, everyone complied, and I cannot remember any problems. Our mothers made numerous cups of tea for the soldiers and were rewarded with tins of fruit, and Carnation milk.

One convoy of Americans left my father with a surprise; the Provost Marshall asked if he could leave a small amount of meat in our garage when they moved out, for us to put out for the dustbin men, but when my father came home later, he found the garage full of sausages and other meats, so he had to get the Public Health Department to deal with it.

The exception to the American convoys was the Free French Soldiers; they remained for a week and despite language problems we got to know them well and were sorry to see them go, but we realised the D-Day Operations were under way, leading eventually to the end of the War, and a lovely party for the children in a nearby field.

Janet Boon-Tilley in wheelbarrow, with Robin Plunkett behind her, in Janet's back garden,
in South Court Avenue, Dorchester, 1943
© Private Collection

Bridport Schools at War

by Fiona Taplin

On the 18th September 1939, Clarissa Rendell, Headmistress of St Mary's Primary School in Gundry Lane reported in the school Log Book: "I have admitted 33 children mostly evacuees from danger zones". The war was only a fortnight old and Bridport Schools were already feeling the impact. Week after week through that autumn, more children arrived; from London, Plymouth, Southampton and other vulnerable areas. By the end of October the numbers were so great that St Mary's and the General Schools were only teaching local children in the mornings, so the evacuees could be taught in the afternoons. Ethel Batchelor, Head of the Junior Department at the General School in King Street organised "optional Nature Study walks, and games," to keep her pupils occupied in the afternoons. Even Bradpole village school had to try to accommodate an influx of thirty-one children, and for such a small school that was not easy.

The situation only eased when temporary evacuation schools were opened at the Baptist Sunday School in Victoria Grove, and the Wesleyan Sunday Schoolroom, South Street. "All available furniture has been lent to seat our visitors in their new buildings," Clarissa Rendell recorded. But it was only a temporary respite for, in November a whole class from a London church school, St Peter's, arrived and had to be accommodated at St Mary's. The St Mary's Nursery Class was an early casualty. From September 1940 all children under five were excluded from school.

Bridport Grammar School might have been expected to cope better, but the building in St Andrews Road was already too small by 1939, so the arrival of evacuees made things very difficult. There were only six classrooms, a library and an art room to house nine classes. The sixth form often found themselves being taught in the corridor outside the Science Room. Extra space was found just down the road in the schoolroom at St Andrews Church. The Church was used for morning assemblies.

Michael Norman, a Grammar School pupil at the time, recalled the arrival of one group of evacuees at Bridport Station. As a member of the local scout troop he was sent to help the volunteer reception party, and escort the children to Allington and East Road where they were to be billeted. He recalls being shocked by the state of some of the children who "really were in rags". In addition to educating the evacuees, the town also cared for war orphans. Battlecombe House on East Road, the former Dower House of the Hyde estate, was taken over and run as an orphanage by the Borough Council Evacuation Committee through the war years.

If the evacuation was one of the most pressing problems schools had to deal with in the early month of the war, it was not ultimately the most testing. Bombing in Bridport was mercifully rare, but the frequent air-raid warnings constantly disrupted school days.

According to the General Senior School Log, Sept 27th 1940 was particularly bad "Air-raids 11:10am – 12:15pm" and again "1:35pm – 2:00pm" Not much work must have been done that day.

All children carried gas masks, and the schools put in place air-raid precautions, though how much use the various trenches that were dug would have been if the town had suffered a major blitz is debateable. Trenches were dug at Skilling, though no one now seems able to remember exactly where. They were only used by St Mary's School for one practice: "The staff were all agreed that it would take too long to get under cover and that a mass of children would be a good target for enemy aeroplanes". It was decided the children would be safer inside the school in the event of an air-raid. To increase safety inside the building the windows were all stripped with brown paper "to prevent splinters of glass flying."

The Grammar School boys were supposed to dig their own trenches along the upper perimeter of the school field bordering Coneygar, but Michael Norman recalls that Mr Jordan, Headmaster of the Grammar School at the time, negotiated a deal with some of the local troops. They completed the trench-digging in return for the use of the boys' football field. While the boys were pleased to avoid the hard labour, their football suffered, as the troops often left the field so churned up, the boys had little but a sea of mud in which to play. Trenches were also dug in the school garden at the General School, though they too do not seem to have been used, other than for practices. When the bombs fell in 1942, the children sheltered under their desks.

Most of these "raids" were false alarms, but two caused extensive damage, and loss of life. They have been described elsewhere in this booklet, so here I will simply record their effect on the schools. The raid that fell behind West Street and seriously damaged the Star Hotel happened during the school holidays. There was minor damage to St Mary's School, which was not repaired by the time the children returned to school in the September due to "shortage of labour", but the air raid on 16th December missed the General Schools by yards. For such a dramatic event, the reports in the Log Books are very brief. Miss Hounsell, in the Infant School Log, records simply: "School bombed today, children took cover immediately on hearing siren. No casualties" and then "very few children present." Jimmy Spenser, Head of the Senior School recorded the time of the air-raid warning at 1:20pm. Ten minutes later the bombs dropped "30 or 40 yards from the school. Much damage was caused to ceilings, roof and windows, so that it was found necessary to close the school until further notice." The school did not reopen until Jan 18th 1943.

The school was incredibly lucky. The devastating explosions totally demolished several houses just east of the King of Belgium Hotel (now The Lord Nelson). The force of the blast was away from the school buildings; otherwise it seems inconceivable that they could have escaped with only the relatively minor damage Mr Spenser records. As it was lunchtime, the majority of children were not on site when the bombs dropped. Several reported seeing the planes fly over the town and hearing the explosions. One recalls debris falling as far south as Back Rivers. St Mary's School did get a proper air-raid shelter, built in the playground, and in 1943 two Morrison Shelters were delivered for the infants, but by this time most of the danger from air-raids was over, so they were used as teacher's desks.

(Cartoon showing a Morrison shelter - May 1941)
"By the way, did you remember to feed the canary?"

The teaching force was affected as many of the men were called up, to be replaced by women, and for those who were left there were additional duties. Mr Jordan, Head of the Grammar School, was a Sergeant in the Home Guard, and CO of the local cadet force which he ran with Mr Richard Inkpen, Head of Allington Senior School. The Grammar School also provided premises for the local ATC (Air Training Corp), which was organised by Tommy Telford, the school Latin master. Dennis Tamblyn, who taught geography, and art and music teacher, Francis Tighe, were called up for war service, and had to exchange the "sober black of an academic gown" for "Air Force blue and khaki" as the School Magazine of 1944 puts it.

Details of St Mary's fund-raising gives an indication of the sums schools raised: £108 5s for *War Weapons Week* in May 1941; £64 4s 1d for *Warship Week* in March 1942 and by 1943 they had collected £150 for the *Wings for Victory* campaign. Grammar School students did holiday work of varying kinds. Senior pupils helped with the post over Christmas, while a large number of pupils spent the 1943 summer holidays flax-pulling, and the Easter and October break, planting, and then lifting potatoes.

VE Day was celebrated by special holidays, parties and parades. Soon swimming lessons at West Bay resumed, and life slowly returned to normal, but, for schools, the post-war years brought change. The Education Act of 1944 raised the school-leaving age to fifteen. A number of schools closed, including the Grammar School, and Allington Secondary Modern School. Sir John Colfox School opened in 1956, and the primaries were radically reorganised. The War was, in every sense, a watershed.

⧂ℛ⧃

NOTE: All the information in the above article is taken from:

1) The Bridport National Mixed School Log Book: 1933-1977: DCRO S.329

2) Taped Interview: Michael Norman: Dorset Schooldays Project. BMS/SCH/05

3) Boys, Girls and Infants General Schools Log Books 1862 -1956: DCRO MIC/R/894

4) Bridport Grammar School Magazine 1944: BMS/ Grammar School File

5) Bradpole School Admissions Register 1944 - 59: DCRO S74/3/3

Extracts from the St. Mary's School Log

Transcribed and edited by Sheila Meaney

Head teacher:
Miss C.M. Rendell

18 September 1939 – We opened this morning after 7 weeks holiday. I have admitted 33 children – mostly evacuees from danger zones. We work 9:00 - 12.15 and do not meet in the afternoon for lessons.

26 October 1939 – We have been unable to carry on the school normally as two rooms in each department are occupied by evacuees – we hope soon to resume ordinary lessons. The classes are getting much bigger. The numbers today are 254.

Evacuees arriving at Bridport Grammar School, 1939
© Private Collection

30 October 1939 – Today our juniors will resume a normal school day as the evacuees have been transferred to the Baptist Sunday Schools. All available furniture has been lent to seat our visitors in their new buildings.

10 November 1939 – On Monday, one class of another London School, St Peters was transferred here and the two upper classes of infants must now occupy one room. Normal lessons can now be carried on but the room is rather crowded and restricts the activities for the young ones.

14 May 1940 – Today we have opened after one day's holiday. All schools were opened because of the serious war situation. I admitted 47 evacuees from St Peter's and Senior Street School, Paddington and 50 other children. The number now on register is 290. Miss Harris who had gone to her home in Wales, was unable to get back on Monday so did not return to duty until Wednesday. Miss Bromfield took her class for the day.

7 June 1940 – On Monday we waited for the siren to blow to get to the trenches. For some reason, the practice was discontinued, but we went as we had arranged. The effort was really disappointing and the staff were all agreed that it would take too long to get under cover and that a mass of children would be a good target for enemy aeroplanes and gave this view to the Rector. As an outcome of communication from the country, we shall stay at school during an air raid instead of leaving the building.

14 June 1940 – Today we have begun to strip each pane of glass in the windows with brown paper to prevent splinters of glass flying about should there be an air raid. Buckets have arrived and these will be filled with sand and water.

3 October 1940 – Mr. Hebdon went for medical exam for Military Service.

14 December 1940 – Mr. Hebdon has joined the R.A.F. We are sorry to lose him as he has been on the staff for 7½ years.

21 May 1941 – Commander Davis of H.M.S. Bridport visited the school and presented us with a picture of the ship. He came too, to thank the children for the gifts of woollies, which we sent to the officers and men in the early part of the year.

14 September 1942 – School re-opened this morning after six weeks holiday. During the early part of the holiday, the buildings were damaged by enemy action. The repairs were delayed owing to shortage of labour.

Gwyneth Hartford (née Harris) who worked at St Mary's during the War. Photographed in 2004.
© Private Collection

17 December 1942 – Yesterday (16th December 1942) we had an air raid. School began late as the "All Clear" had not gone. We had a poor attendance and during the afternoon many parents called to see if their children were safe, as bombs had fallen at the other end of the town and there were casualties and much damage. Our building was undamaged.

14 May 1943 – Mr Armstrong, Mr Northover head of A.R.P. and the County Architect called this morning re: A.R.P. shelters. They visited the Infant Department and decided that nine Morrison Shelters would accommodate the infants. The juniors will use the two cloakrooms which were converted into shelters in 1940.

15 July 1943 – The Morrison Shelters arrived last Saturday. Three were erected in each of the infant rooms.

12 September 1944 – The school nurse came this morning. She found a clean school except two evacuees, who received a warning but were not excluded.

11 May 1945 – The school was closed for V.E. celebrations.

14 January 1946 – One canteen helper has left as her husband is returning from Germany.

5 May 1946 – School re-opened today and Mr Hebdon returned after a long absence in the R.A.F.

Postscript

One of the first evacuees from Senior Street School was a Charlie Wilson . . . Do the words Great, Train and Robbery ring a bell?

Bridport News during the War

by Holly Robinson

Recent events in Iraq have changed how wars and their consequences are reported forever. We now take for granted how easy it is to find out about anything we want on the internet. We can look up the latest news on teletext or Ceefax, or pick from hundreds of satellite and terrestrial TV stations to view.

Rolling 24-hour news not only shows our troops in action across the globe but, as was witnessed in Iraq, often it is able to reveal the devastating consequences of air strikes and enemy engagements from the ground even before the authorities can work out if they hit the right target, or at least decide whether to keep quiet for tactical reasons. Perhaps even more remarkably we can sit at home watching the war play out from all sides, with TV stations and press conferences representing all involved. Now wars are played out bullet by bullet, bomb by bomb, in the full glare of the watching public.

Leading Article in the Bridport News,
Friday September 8, 1939

For many it is hard to imagine a time without instant access to news and information or the ability to email, text or call a loved one on a mobile phone for immediate response.

During the Second World War censored radio reports, and newspapers were among the few ways to get information out to the masses. Information was vital with new laws, rationing, and black outs to explain, not to mention the threat of bombing and possible invasion. The regional press and newspapers like the *Bridport News* had a key role to play in the war effort. While newspapers continued to carry local news and the latest births, deaths and marriages, and sports results, it was also necessary to let people know what they could, and should, do to help.

The official declaration of war is carried on page 7 of the *Bridport News* dated September 8, 1939 "Britain and France at war with Nazi Germany". A message from the King and a speech by Prime Minister Neville Chamberlain are reported along with instructions for motorists of what to do during an air raid and reports that London was calm during the first air raid warning.

In the same edition as stories on the West Bay sewage scheme being dropped and the results of the 1939 Melplash Show there are pieces about the setting up of a new register of all Britons, a report on how to send parcels to the troops and adverts on the wisdom of making a will. It is also noted that all short term prisoners with less than three months to serve would be freed. Regular features included lists of firms carrying out work of "national importance for able bodied workers".

Advice on the war effort included reports such as "Your garden versus U-boats" encouraging people to grow more vegetables and explanations about what items were to be rationed and how to get them. Even advertisers had to become inventive to sell their wares; Wrigley's chewing gum is revealed as "first-aid for the nerves" particularly for smokers unable to light up in their factories or in the air raid shelter.

At the start of the war the *Bridport News* continued in its eight page broadsheet format but with calls to save paper, and many items becoming more difficult to come by, the war brought with it a reduction to four pages.

Unlike today, there was no continuing stream of news from the front, or tales of the latest bombs to hit London or closer to home, but instead every now and then a few inches of type would declare the latest happenings, often including a report of heroism by a local boy doing his duty.

War coverage was mainly centred on advice and information, much of it in the form of adverts from bodies like the Ministry of Information proclaiming such words of wisdom as "Keep to the left" (to avoid accidents between pedestrians in the blackout) or "Guard your tongue" to avoid secrets falling into enemy hands.

News of evacuees and how to help them was a regular feature of papers in the war years, alongside amusing anecdotes such as the boy who saw Hitler on a bus in Sherborne.

There were regular attempts to lighten the mood at home with Christmas editions of the newspaper featuring lists of amusing experiments to try, and instructions on how to make shadows in the shape of various animals.

Newspapers throughout the war were peppered with "handy tips" designed to keep the household running: food facts leap from the page with recipes showing how to make 'appetising' meals from the resources available. There were warnings that "potatoes are precious" and ways to make "new style" scotch eggs without the usual ingredients. The Ministry of Food gave out regular advice designed to persuade home cooks they were doing fine in these hard times. Topics included reports on how to feed mother and baby during rationing, and what to do when youngsters turned five and needed a different ration book. There were also upbeat advertising to encourage families to make use of the processed alternatives on offer: "Dried eggs are the finest eggs with the shell and water taken away. White and yolk are blended together so you get the same mixture every time."

News pages carried warnings about the consumption of gas and electricity, and the need to conserve everything.

Adverts headlined "Now is your chance", "What do I do?" scream from the pages, alongside apologies from firms unable to meet their usual commitments. *Farmers Weekly* was among the publications unable to get all their usual copies printed due to paper rationing.

But firms also had to look to the future and think of what happens next. An advert for the Westminster Bank reads: "Looking ahead – the post war world will need business initiative, foresight and courage. The services of the Westminster Bank are at the disposal of all those who are or will be engaged in the task of reconstruction and expansion both at home an overseas. Credit facilities will be readily available to meet the requirements of all classes of trustworthy borrowers."

The Ministry of Information had many messages to get out, not least about keeping healthy and helping the war effort. "Sneezing to the danger of the public, and coughing without due care and attention are common offences these days," the ministry warns. "They rob the war effort of thousands of working hours just when the final spurt to victory is needed."

THE SEASON'S COMPLIMENTS

There are some things the war can't stop. It can't stop Christmas cheerfulness. It can't stop the ring of laughter, and kindly greetings. It can't stop our preference for the glass of beer which makes for cheeriness and good fellowship.

In sad days and glad days beer has played its part. It was the drink of our forefathers in the cheery "old fashioned" Christmasses of days gone by. It has heartened us in the last few months. Now let it keep to the fore kindliness and good humour and happiness—at *this* Christmastime.

Whether it be ale or stout or mild or bitter — stick to British beer this Christmas. It will keep you in good form, sharpen up your appetite, make you hearty and healthy.

At the pub or for the family party at home, beer is best. It will help to make — a happy Christmas.

Beer Advertisement in the Bridport News, Friday December 22, 1939

The long-awaited day of Victory in Europe may have brought with it flags and bunting and a tea party for 1,200 school children, but it was not the end.

While front page classified adverts reveals information about thanksgiving services and, special meetings, and many village dances, they sit alongside a large advert from the Ministry of Information shouting "Thanks, but don't stop ..... The need is as urgent as ever for waste paper and rag and bone salvage for the fighting men."

Inside are food facts on yet more "new" ways of using dried eggs, plus the good news that more children aged five to 10 would get orange juice in May and June.

Victory is revealed in two columns on the back page of the *Bridport News* on May 11, 1945: "Victory! Shout it from the housetops and across the fields and overseas. Let it resound from end to end of the earth. Let it echo down the arches of the years. Cry it jubilantly in your hearts and whisper it humbly in your prayers. This is a victory greater than all the triumphs of Alexander and Julius Caesar, of Saladin and Genghis Kahan, of Napoleon and Wellington. No battle honours inscribed on our centuries-old colours can compare with this."

Bridport Mayor Councillor S.J. Gale said: "The month and years which come after VE Day will prove whether we are equal to this great responsibility of helping to rebuild the world. "War must be outlawed, industrial strife and poverty which have laid an ugly mark on the face of the earth must be banished also. That, I am convinced, rests in your hands."

The back page of the *Bridport News* of August 17, 1945 announced: "Peace Comes at Last", but victory was not the end of the hardship as future papers would show for months to come, and as if by warning there sitting side by side with the final victory report is a one column piece devoted to: "making the most of cabbage."

Local Hero – Bill Budden

by Rene Gerryts

Bill Budden's wife Vera always knew when something big was about to happen during War.

She wouldn't hear from Bill as his camp in Broadwell in Oxfordshire was sealed off from contact with the outside world, no-one was allowed in or out and no post was allowed through. She said: "They had to bake their own bread and had to suddenly become self sufficient."

What she probably could not imagine was the magnitude of what was about to happen on the shores of France just over 60 years ago; the biggest invasion the world had ever seen.

This year's 60th anniversary of the end of the World War II is perhaps our last opportunity to hear first-hand about the extraordinary feats of courage and endurance undertaken by ordinary men and women.

Bill Budden, from Loders, was one of those ordinary men and even now he doesn't want a fuss

Bill Budden photograph taken during World War 2
© Private collection

made of the part he played. In fact it's a job to get him to agree to be interviewed at all. Bill was working at Pymore Mill when war broke out and he figured if he waited to be called up he'd end up in the army so he joined on his 19th birthday in March 1940.

> *I got bored with work and preferred the RAF to the possibility of being conscripted into the army. I didn't really consider the problems I just felt I would prefer the RAF so I went early to avoid being conscripted. I had no idea what it was going to be like.*
>
> *At first there was very little happening. Paris had fallen. I was not called in until the end of May. I did ground duties for the first 12 months waiting for flying training.*

He went for his flying navigation training in Canada in 1941 and was there six months learning about navigation, bombing, gunnery and anti-submarine sweeping, which could involve 11-hour flights flying 300ft above the sea. He was in coastal and then bomber command and by June 1942 was posted to the Middle East for night bombing raids.

> *After Dunkirk we expected Hitler might invade. We were lucky he decided to go for Russia instead. It would have been curtains for us otherwise.*
>
> *People in England might have known that we were going to invade but luckily it*

came as a surprise to the Germans, and, nearly not so luckily, to our friends in the French Resistance.

Plans included the dropping by parachute at night of French speaking British officers of the Special Operations Executive who were brave enough to undertake the task of reporting back enemy troop concentrations and the briefing of the French underground forces as to what was planned. Their lives were in danger from both German and French collaborators. One officer reported that when the landing was postponed one day because of weather, the French considered shooting him as an impostor!

Bill started training with Dakota aircraft for the parachute drops and with glider tugging for six months before D-Day. The glider pilots were army personnel and they had very little training. The gliders were used to carry jeeps, guns and troops.

They took the heaviest losses. They would land and blow the nose off, walk out and abandon the plane.

Bill was the map reader and was one of the first in with the airborne forces. They had to drop 600 paratroopers from Dakotas on a bridge on the River Orne at Ranville at 01:05. About fifty planes were dropping at Ranville.

The sky was full of aircraft. RAF bombers were bombing Caen.

Our drop time was 01:05 behind enemy lines. The RAF had already dropped five gliders on Pegasus Bridge a few minutes earlier. We turned and came back out and had to go in again because the Major in charge refused to jump, he said we were flying too low. We were working with an altimeter which was accurate and we knew we were flying at exactly 600ft but it was his prerogative. If they jump and they are too low they get killed. We came back later that day with a glider full of airborne forces.

I suppose I was thinking I was glad I was not jumping. They were probably excited and apprehensive. They knew they were in a very dangerous situation.

It was dark when Bill made the first of many trips that day, but they heard on the radio about the carnage on the beaches and saw the channel solid with ships as far as they eye could see. They knew about the men drowning as they were dropped off in too deep water, about the equipment lost and the slaughter, particularly where the Americans landed on Omaha and Utah beaches.

The opposition from the German armies was very heavy. Losses were severe. The Americans had thousands killed on the first day; they never left the beach. They had the greatest battle, a steep beach towards the land and sea too rough for some landing craft to beach. Soldiers had to jump into deep water, laden with packs, rifles, and ammunition. It was carnage. They had no chance and it took a month to break out and move west before any aircraft could land to bring out wounded.

As the allied forces gradually made advances after D-Day, Bill was busy re-supplying the army with medical supplies, ammunition, and fuel. Later on he was bringing back prisoners of war and those lucky enough to survive the concentration camps.

> We brought back people released from Belsen which I would not want to do again. That was one of the worst things, they were dying like flies. It was in the British papers by then but it was still a shock to see them. They looked like skeletons.

> We took them to Luneburger Heath in Germany which was an exchange base for POWs of all nationalities. There was nothing there just that Dakotas could land there easily. We dropped them in hordes, there could be quarter of a million people there at any one time all wanting to be taken somewhere.

> It would have been a dismal failure without the Americans. They had the equipment; they had the power and the money. We didn't stand a chance without them.

Despite all that the war was a good time for many men. Bill met his wife who was in the WAF at Beaulieu in August 1943.

> I was an instructor in low level bombing then. Vera was a mechanic on bomber aircraft. She changed as soon as she could and got herself re-mustered as a secretary. She thought being a mechanic was dirty and cold.

> I thought it was the best years of my life. I had to make no decisions, they were all made for you, and pay came regularly with no fear of redundancy.

After the war Bill worked for Gundrys and started Bridport Aviation products until his retirement.

Beaminster's Forgotten Army

Extract from 'Dorset Attacked Dorset Defended' by kind permission of the author, Robin Pearce.

The Women's Land Army was formed in June 1939, the county headquarters for Dorset were at County Hall and the county organiser was Dorothy Evans. The uniform was a fawn shirt with a green and red tie bearing the initials W.L.A. in yellow letters. This was worn with a pair of fawn knee-breeches. Long woollen stockings were turned down at the knee, just covering the hem of the breeches. Over the shirt they wore a green sweater on which was pinned the W.L.A. badge. On the left arm they wore a yellow felt armband.

The girls worked a 48 hour week and were paid a shilling (5p) an hour. The pay rate rose during the war and the forewomen in hostels were paid an extra ten shillings (50p) for their responsibilities. They had a week's leave every six months and some who were a long way from home would take two weeks together each year. Unlike other womens' services, they were not paid any 'demobilization' gratuity when they left after the war. They were not allowed into the NAAFIs (the Navy, Army and Air Force Institutes) and after the war were not allowed to take part in Remembrance Day parades.

Food production was maintained and even increased when the girls took over the work of thousands of young men called up for service. They put in tremendous effort and worked efficiently whether they were milking cows, clearing rough down-land for cereal production, pulling flax, hoeing, haymaking, threshing, fruit picking or rat catching.

The Beaminster hostel was a long wooden building with an extension at the rear. It stood in the field next to Whatley Mill, near the end of the lane which starts at Holy Trinity Church. The building consisted of a dormitory with rows of double bunk-beds for the thirty girls, a dining/recreation room, the kitchen and warden's quarters. There was a small sick bay which would be used for visitors if necessary. At the back was the extension with the wash-room, baths and the laundry.

The food provided for the girls was good. Doris Britton said that they ate 'like horses and there were always second helpings'. In the evening they took it in turns to make the sandwiches for the next day. The bread from the local bakery was the best some of them had ever tasted. Having started with a cooked breakfast and taking a packed lunch and flask of tea, they were ready for a strenuous day's work. Of the 696 hostels throughout the country Beaminster was one of the best.

Eirwen Evans, Rosemary Lawford, Marjorie Cheeseman, and Mary Andrews outside the Beaminster Hostel.
© Private Collection

The warden, Miss Ethel Catchpole, had few rules and was respected by the girls. She had to keep a register and ensure the girls were in by 10pm, unless they had permission to stay out late. There were plenty of dances in the area especially after the Americans arrived in 1943. They were issued with bikes and could explore the country-side, even though finding the way without road signs could be difficult. (These had been removed because of the threat of invasion). Some of the Land Girls like Doris Brittan and Gwendoline Notley were employed by the farmers, but still under the authority of the Land Army. It was the girls in the hostels who were controlled by 'War Ag' (War Agriculture Executive Committees). In some hostels, like Beaminster, where the forewomen had a good relationship with many farmers in the area, the work was largely arranged by them. In this way they could often manage to avoid the farmers who exploited them.

The girls in Beaminster came from all over the country and some met future husbands and all made lifelong friends. There are no monuments or memorials to them in Dorset but those who travel on the A35 between Bridport and Dorchester can still see evidence of their work in the wide prairie-like fields on either side.

Memories of West Dorset People in World War II

by Jane Ferentzi-Sheppard

Ronald Sheppard

Ronald Sheppard, was a booking clerk at Dorchester South, Station from 1939 until he was called up in 1941. His father and brother were also serving on the railway at the same time.

This extract is part of an interview with my father Ronald William Sheppard in March 2000. He is talking about his experiences on the railways, and about the early part of World War II in Dorchester.

So when war broke out, what happened really to change your everyday life in the booking office?

Well, we had an emphasis on military traffic and on the night shift, of course, trains used to become quite late when there were

Ronald, Charles Snr, and Charles Jnr Sheppard,
Dorchester Home Guard, 1940
© Private Collection

enemy raids on London or Southampton or anywhere that affected our railway system. We were alert to that and also, of course, like other people we were persuaded to join defence organisations, and I joined the L.D.V. (the Local Defence Volunteers), that was before it became the Home Guard. We used to do certain duties at night and guard the station. It was a bit comical really, because we didn't have a great deal of armaments. We started with carrying a pole around and then we were later issued with rifles. We used to parade, have drills and that kind of thing, and our regular guard duties, so sometimes I expect we were pretty sleepy in the office when it came around.

Did you have a uniform for that?

Yes. First of all we had a sort of a denim uniform and then later on a real army-style material. We had an overcoat, just like the Army, only we had a badge round our arms with Home Guard on there or Local Defence Volunteer.

Was there a big increase in troop movement?

Well, there were troops always on the move going out from Dorchester and we had troops returned after the fall of Dunkirk and trains coming in with all the poor soldiers aboard. That was the thing. We had different tickets, individual tickets weren't issued to the soldiers if they were on duty, they used to travel on the travel warrants, you see, and we used to collect all the travel warrants and send them up and I suppose the War Department gave us so much per journey.

And when were you called up?

Well, I served there until I was called up in October 1941, and I was called up to the R.A.F., which I had been waiting for rather urgently. Then I had to go away and report at Blackpool and I did my training. I trained in the R.A.F. as a wireless operator specialising first in direction finding and then later on, taking a wireless mechanics course so I became a W.O.M., (a Wireless Operator Mechanic), and I really enjoyed my service in the Air Force.

My Dad died in October 2003.

✿

Audrey Stone (née Lake)

Audrey Stone. Audrey grew up in Dorchester and was 15 when this event happened. She later worked at County Hall.

Dorchester 8am 4 July 1940

I left home to catch the train to Weymouth, joining friends who had already travelled from Wareham and Swanage. We were on our way to the South Dorset Technical College. The journey was uneventful. As usual we threw yesterday's newspaper from the carriage to the sentry on guard at the Ridgeway Tunnel, something we did everyday.

On arrival at Weymouth we immediately knew that this was no ordinary day. At 8.40 am a flight of Junker bombers attacked the 'Foylebank' in Weymouth Harbour. The sky was black with smoke and there was a great deal of noise. We ran down Park Street, across Westham Bridge

Audrey Stone (née Lake) at County Hall, Dorchester, 1945.
© Private Collection

and along the marsh and sheltered under the railway bridge which linked Weymouth Station across the Back water. Somebody said 'lets run for it' we did and climbed up the bank (where the houses named College Heights now stand) and into the school grounds. We were then marshalled into open trenches with our feet on the duckboards for a good part of the day. There was no overhead attack and we were safe. We caught the 4.40 pm train back home – it left on time in spite of the horror of that day.

Leading Seaman Jack Mantle defending the 'Foylebank' won his VC, collapsing at his gun, mortally wounded. It was still only 8.48 am. He is buried in the Portland Naval Cemetery. For more information see *Weymouth and Portland at War – Countdown to D-Day* by Maureen Attwoll & Denise Harrison.

✿

Kathleen Sheppard (née Murray)

Kathleen lived in Dorchester from 1943 and worked at County Hall.

I did A.R.P. (Air Raid Precaution) duty at County Hall, Dorchester in 1943 when I was 16. I volunteered and we were given a training day in Fordington. We were given a helmet, arm band and a gas mask in a bag. I remember the men wore blue boiler suits. My friend Joan and I did one night a week from 7.30 pm to 6.00 am. We stayed in rooms in County Hall, our room was partitioned off with small cubicles for us to sleep in. We had two older men and a lad with us. The two men went off to the local pub but came running back as soon as the siren went off.

Kathleen Sheppard (née Murray)
Dorchester 1944
© Private Collection

It was wonderful to see Dorchester and the surrounding area at night from the flat roof of County Hall. We could see the search lights to the north of the town. We were coming home one morning and were stopped by a policeman asking where we had been. We showed him our arm bands and were told to hurry home for our breakfast!

I enjoyed my time in the ARP, it was good fun and we were doing our bit.

☙❧

Dawn Gould (née Yardy)

Dawn Gould grew up in Weymouth, enjoying the outdoor life of living by the sea. She was a good swimmer and enjoyed dancing and singing. In 1943 Dawn became an ARP (Air Raid Precaution) messenger riding around Weymouth on her father's racing bike. Her life, like so many other young girls changed with the 'friendly invasion' of the Americans in the autumn of 1943. An entry in her diary reads *The Yanks are coming!*.

The first impression of these GIs was the perfume of the lotion and Menen Talc which they wore. We in Britain had never heard of aftershave then. They also used scented soap, which had been unobtainable here for a long time. We soon realised we knew very little about these men but did our best to make them welcome. The look and feel of their uniforms was so very different from the rough hairy material which British servicemen wore. They also had well cared for and gleaming white teeth. We soon realised that although we all spoke English there could be some serious misunderstandings in the way we used it… and Wow! Could they dance!

The arrival of the US 1st Division in Dorset swelled the population of the county by about 80,000. This brought lots of shows and famous stars to entertain the troops and local musicians and singers joined in. Dawn sang and danced all over Dorset, always accompanied by her Mum who acted as a chaperone for her and her friends. Still only sixteen she was singing at the Regent one evening at the end of 1943 when a young GI, on duty as a Military Policeman, spotted her and found out who she was and that she was there with her mother.

He introduced himself to my mother and asked if he could take me out on a date. My mother asked him if he was a gentleman, he replied, 'Yes Ma'am, a Southern gentleman'. The next evening we went to the cinema. This was my first real date.

My first love was tall dark and handsome and a full-blooded Choctaw Indian. Stewart had been brought up with his two sisters in a strict Catholic orphanage in Louisiana. He was stationed at

Dawn and Stewart
© Private Collection

Broadmayne with the 2nd Battalion, 18th Infantry Regiment of the 1st Division and we saw each other as much as possible in the months to come. We talked for hours about all sorts of things and made plans for the future planning a life in New Orleans. Looking back we were very different, he a strict Catholic and me a Chapel Methodist, he did not dance and I loved dancing especially jitterbug, but at seventeen these things were not important.

On 8th May 1944 Dawn and Stewart Koger became engaged and it was announced in the Dorset Evening Echo, hundreds of other couples were doing the same thing as the build up to D-Day began.

The last time I saw Stewart he was waving goodbye from the back of a truck taking him back to camp at Broadmayne. He went over on D-Day and landed at Omaha Beach. I do not know when he was killed, but my letters were returned by the American Post Office marked Deceased Return to Sender, as I was not next of kin. I heard no more. I did hear from his sister to say how sorry she was. I continued to be a hostess at the American Red Cross Club in St Thomas St, Weymouth and in September 1944 I went to work at the Ministry of Agriculture & Fisheries, in County Hall, Dorchester and joined the Women's

Land Army. The events and pain of 1944 never completely leave one.

Dawn Gould has become a focal point for Ex GIs especially those from the 'Big Red One'. War brides, researchers and historians often visit and exchange memories and stories of that eventful time, which touched so many people's lives here in Dorset.

---------- MUSIC BY ----------

THE 18TH INFANTRY "GIN SLINGERS"

THEY SLING WHILE YOU SWING

DATE -- Tuesday, April 11, 1944
TIME -- 8 P. M.
PLACE -- Poundbury Camp West
UNIFORM -- "As You Is"

Guerrillas in the Beaminster Woods

by Bob Pearson

After the evacuation of British forces from Dunkirk in 1940, Britain was in imminent danger of a German invasion. Winston Churchill famously vowed that we would fight them not just on the seas and in the air, also "in the fields" and "in the hills". True to his word, Churchill ordered the setting up of a secret guerrilla-type movement, with selected personnel trained in the art of specialised resistance fighting.

Small groups of civilian volunteers of six to eight men were recruited to carry out sabotage, guerrilla warfare and spying from behind enemy lines in this country. The groups, called Auxiliary Units, were to be as independent of one another as possible and were to operate from underground bases.

Initially the units were recruited from countrymen, farmers, foresters and gamekeepers; those who had such an intimate knowledge of their own areas that they could move around at night. Just such a unit was organised in Beaminster and its existence remained secret, even from the families of the volunteers, for many years.

There is just one surviving member of the six-man Beaminster unit, which was led by John Wakely of Cherry Cott Farm, and that is 90 year-old George Raymond, a retired local farmer. George is a quietly spoken person with a ready sense of humour. He was prepared to talk about this strange episode in his life for the *Beaminster Society* magazine. One sensed, during the conversation, that he was being typically modest about the importance of this band of countrymen, who would have been in the last-ditch stand against the enemy, perhaps buying sufficient time for an unlikely counter-attack by Allied forces to take place.

Before beginning George's personal account, mention should be made of the fascinating means by which key personnel of the Auxiliary Units were vetted before their training began at Coleshill House (renamed the Auxiliary Gateway), near Highworth in Wiltshire.

Stamp of approval

In a scenario of which Ian Fleming, creator of James Bond, would have approved (indeed, his brother Peter helped to organise the whole operation), recruits would first have to report to a Mrs Mabel Stranks, the postmistress at Highworth. She was a 58 year-old, grey-haired unassuming widow, the sort of person least likely to front a spy organisation.

When a hand-picked recruit arrived at the Post Office, in Beaminster's case this was John Wakely, he would ask for Mrs Stranks and give a prearranged password. She would then make a number of telephone calls to senior military sources to state whether she considered him to be "official" or "unofficial". The former would be collected and taken by car to the Auxiliary Gateway, while the unfortunate latter would be taken elsewhere, no doubt for intensive interrogation.

Mabel Stranks never spoke of her role until close to her death in 1971, and even declined an offer to take part in a documentary about her service. A plaque has since been placed on the old Post Office at Highworth by the local town council, as a lasting memorial to this extraordinary lady.

The underground operational base of the Beaminster Auxiliary Unit. The concealed entrance leads to steps going down into the main chamber. At the rear is an air vent, which could have been used as an escape route.
© Photograph by courtesy of Jim House

Beaminster's fighting unit

On his return, after having been trained in guerrilla warfare, John Wakely began recruiting for Beaminster's Auxiliary Unit from among those he could trust. Members were to wear Home Guard uniforms as a deception and were issued with a badge bearing the number 203, which represented the Southern Counties, a fighting knife and a revolver, as well as explosives, timing devices and detonators. Here we continue with George Raymond's memories of the time:

I was recruited by John Wakely in the spring of 1940. John, who was our sergeant and led the unit, also recruited Stanley Bale from Axnoller, my brother Ernest Frank Ivory, who lived in Fleet Street, and Douglas Perkins, who lived in one of the cottages in Fleet Street now owned by the Abbot Brown printing works. Frank and Doug were called up to join the regular army after about a year, and they were replaced by Henry Higgins of Northfield Farm and Vic Downton from Shortmoor, who also worked at Northfield Farm.

Our OB, or operational base, was originally in a disused lime-kiln in some woods above Ebenezer Cottage in Stintsford Lane, up near the picnic site. We had to crawl through the tiny opening to get inside. After that, the army constructed a special underground chamber for us, with the entrance hidden by bushes. There was also a vent for the supply of fresh air. I remember John saying that his father complained about the army causing chaos in the woods, but of course John couldn't tell him that it was all for our benefit.

The chamber was divided into two rooms, one for our use and the other one, which I never saw opened, for equipment.

It is likely that the equipment room, or perhaps a large cupboard, that George refers to held operational stores and rations sufficient for 14 days, which was the anticipated useful life of the units in action. After that period, and if undiscovered, the men would revert to a non-operational role as civilians. This was the system for similar Auxiliary Units elsewhere. No doubt, John Wakely held the key to this store.

I do remember that when we were eventually disbanded everything in the OB had to be returned, including a large jar of rum, John said it shouldn't all go to waste and took several healthy swigs from it!

Nocturnal manoeuvres

We were trained by John to approach "German-held" farms at night, to destroy any vehicles – German or otherwise – with a plastic explosive that looked like a string of sausages. You could wrap it halfway around a tree, for example, to fell the tree across a road as a barrier to enemy vehicles. We practised the technique on one or two trees and it was very successful. Another use was to attach it to the axles or undercarriages of enemy vehicles to destroy them.

We operated in pairs, as silent and unseen as possible, to reduce the risk of being caught but we had to split up to get home after exercises. Early one morning, on my way back from one of these night missions, I ran into a couple of unexpected regular soldiers posted as sentries to catch us, but I managed to convince them that I was a farmer on my way to milk the cows. John was very impressed that I had avoided the trap.

We were issued with a combat knife, a revolver and hand grenades. These were only to be used in an emergency, as the main intention was to make a sabotage attempt and then withdraw immediately.

Although we knew there were other units operating in Dorset, we didn't know exactly whereabouts or who the men were. This was a precaution in case we were captured and tortured for information. For the same reason, we told our parents we were in the Home Guard, which would be the story if the Germans caught us. Under interrogation one could "break down" and admit being members of the Home Guard, which hopefully would not have warranted the same punishment as being saboteurs.

Another of our activities was to reconnoitre by night any likely places the Germans might take over, such as Mapperton House. We learned how to place trip-wires with small explosives attached, so that if enemy vehicles set them off we would know they were around.

Lighter moments

We took our training very seriously, but there were some very funny incidents, if you bear in mind that we were also just a group of youngsters out for the night. Remember that Frank Ivory wasn't as used to gallivanting around the countryside as we farmers were, at least at first. One dark night, John lost patience and shouted at him for making too much noise while crawling through a hedge. Poor Frank had got stuck and was just trying to free himself.

John got into trouble with the authorities on one occasion. We were returning back from training one night, approaching the town from the Bridport direction. When we reached the old police station, where the youth club is now, he decided that Beaminster was a bit too quiet and lit up a thunderflash – a sort of imitation hand grenade like a big firework – which exploded with a huge bang. We scarpered, but eventually John had to own up.

Licensed to kill

After our local training was finished, we were sent to the area headquarters at Melcombe Bingham for a weekend, to be assessed and to undergo further training. To get there, Frank Ivory borrowed Dr Hope-Simpson's sports car, which was very well known in Beaminster. As we started out very late and Frank was anxious we should arrive in time, it was quite a hair-raising journey, I can tell you, and we all felt lucky to have arrived in one piece.

They were pleased with us at HQ and said that John had trained us well. We had to sleep rough while we were there and we were given plenty of revolver practice and learnt a few more stealth tactics. We were also taught how to silently dispatch a German sentry with our knives. I remember being almost deaf for several days after so much firing.

We were disbanded in 1944, by which time the emergency was over and the tide had turned against the enemy. We all just went back to our normal routines as if nothing had happened.

I gave my cap and uniform to the Beaminster Museum in 2001, but all the other equipment had to be handed in. John Wakely managed to hang on to his badge somehow. I expect he told the authorities he had lost it. John's widow, Kate, has also donated it to the Museum, so they've now got a uniform and a badge together.

John Wakeley's Auxiliary Unit of hand-picked and specially trained men were never called into action, as the Nazi menace didn't materialise. The town should, however, be proud that these Beaminster men were brave enough to volunteer for this exceedingly dangerous operation.

The names of the Beaminster folk who served in both World Wars, some badly wounded and others unfortunately never to return, are to be seen in the wall by St Mary's Church gate.

The writer would like to thank George Raymond for sharing his experiences of his time in the Beaminster Auxiliary Unit, and Jim House for providing information on the setting up of Churchill's secret guerrilla movement.

The Yukon Exercise

by Sheila Meaney

Few people in the Bridport area today, realise that the coast between Burton Bradstock and Eype, was the scene of major military activity in June of 1942. On two separate days, June 12th and June 23rd, over 4,000 troops and 58 tanks were landed at different points along the coast in a rehearsal for an operation being planned for later in the year; a raid on the French town of Dieppe.

The decision to launch a raid on Dieppe has always been the subject of controversy. More than sixty years later the subject still arouses heated discussion and disagreement, but in the early part of 1942, it was clear that with the German invasion of Russia, that country was looking to Britain and her allies to launch a diversionary action in Europe, which would take pressure off them. While nothing on the scale of an 'invasion' was considered, it was determined that a large 'Raid' would be organised, which would test the German defences along the French coast while at the same time assessing the

Canadian Troops at West Bay, Bridport, during the Yukon Exercise.
© Photograph by courtesy of the Public Archives Canada

Allies ability to launch a large 'combined operation' involving all three Services from allied countries.

So why was the coastal area near Bridport chosen for the Yukon exercise?

Any resident of West Dorset sailing into Dieppe harbour, will feel 'at home' – the shape and form of the coastline, the gradient of the cliffs, the small beaches stretching away on either side of the harbour and the pebbly texture of the beaches all have a very familiar feel and it was this physical similarity which led to the selection of the Bridport area for the rehearsal exercises.

At the initial planning stages, it was agreed that a direct, single assault on the heavily defended port of Dieppe would be an extremely hazardous and difficult undertaking and that to have any chance of success additional landings would have to be made on the flanks of the port, to destroy the coastal defence batteries.

To coordinate and synchronise landings on all these beaches and then organise the subsequent withdrawal of personnel and equipment at the end of the raid, would be an immense logistical problem; challenging and fraught with difficulties, and so the Yukon Exercise was planned. It provided an opportunity to rehearse the projected assault, combining all the elements that would constitute the planned raid on Dieppe.

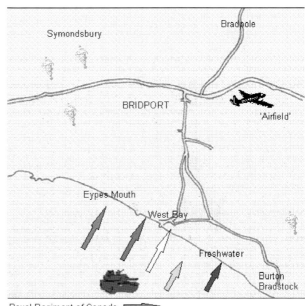

Yukon Exercise: June 1942.
A simplified sketch map to show the landing beaches of the
Canadian Second Division

Royal Regiment of Canada
Essex Scottish
Royal Hamilton Light Infantry
South Saskatchewan Rifles
Camerons of Canada
14th Tank Battalion. 'Calgary Tanks'.

The troops of the Canadian 2nd Division, under the command of Major-General Roberts, were assigned to the Raid and the Royal Navy, Royal Marine Commandos, Royal Naval Commandos, the R.A.F and a small detachment of U.S. Rangers fought alongside them.

Many of the Canadian forces had been in Britain since 1940, and were mainly young, untried and untested, but in May they embarked upon intensive training around the Isle of Wight. They worked at improving their stamina whilst carrying assault loads, ascending cliff like gradients, they engaged in street fighting, and practised artillery skills and assault procedures as well as training for an orderly re-embarkation withdrawal from the beaches.

It was decided that 'YUKON' – the dry run for the Dieppe raid, would take place on June 12th. Troops would commence landing at dawn, undertake their tasks and then re-embark and return to base in the late afternoon.

In the week prior to the exercise, a plane had flown up and down the Dorset coast taking a series of aerial photographs from Cogden Beach down to Seatown, gathering information about the coastline and the area inland to be used in briefing procedures. At the same time, a Combined Operations staff meeting was taking place at West Bay. The stage was being set for the exercise.

The plan, as all plans are, was straightforward

In its simplest terms, defending forces (German in exercise terms) were deployed along the coast from Seatown to Burton Bradstock and in Bridport and the surrounding area, including Walditch, Wanderwell, Watton and Coneygar. The troops in these positions were manning coastal batteries, inland gun emplacements and defending key designated locations. Their Divisional Headquarters and a (fictitious) airfield at Bradpole were central to the proceedings.

The physical layout of the key beaches and defensive positions, replicated in notional terms, the conditions and terrain that the troops would find on the French coast around Dieppe.

For Yukon, West Bay and its harbour became Dieppe, its enclosing East and West beaches designated White and Red beaches respectively. To the west, Eypesmouth, was Puits (Puys), codename, Blue Beach. To the east, Burton Freshwater beach was Poirville, codename, Green beach. Bradpole and its 'airfield' became Arques, the site of the real airfield on the outskirts of Dieppe.

Eypesmouth (Blue beach) and Freshwater (Green beach) were to see the first wave of troops at dawn. The Royal Regiment of Canada and the South Saskatchewan Rifles undertook the flanking assaults, putting the gun batteries in their respective areas out of action and then sweeping inland, clearing Burton Bradstock, Eype and Watton of any opposition, preparing the way for the second wave of landings at West Bay.

Puits (Puys) Beach, France

An hour after the initial landings, the Essex, Scottish and the Royal Hamilton Light Infantry launched their frontal assault on West Bay, followed up by the 14th Tank Battalion, the 'Calgary Tanks' who supported the ground actions and then moved on through Bridport and Bothenhampton with their new Churchill tanks, to control the roads to and from Bradpole, while supporting the final players in the exercise, the Camerons of Canada, whose task was to capture the Divisional Headquarters and the airfield.

Mission accomplished, all these companies returned to West Bay, Red and White beaches, while the Fusiliers Mont Royale held a covering defensive position to enable embarkation to proceed.

The best laid plans... so they say...

The Yukon exercise on the 12th of June was a disaster; poor communications, insufficient intelligence regarding the landing sites, over ambitious time scale, lack of combined training activities and inadequate provision of basic equipment, all contributed to a series of errors which compounded as the day went on.

Some 4,000 troops were landed, most of them late and in daylight so the element of surprise, so vital to the operation, was lost. In two locations the troops were landed on the wrong beach because visual identification made from the sea was incorrect. Those aerial photographs, taken directly above the beaches, gave little detail of the shape of the cliffs and beaches when viewed from off shore. The Royal Regiment landed too far west and had to get from Seatown to Eypesmouth before they could move against their designated targets. The South Saskatchewan Rifles were landed too far east, at Burton Bradstock, where no path had been cleared through the minefield on the beach. Burton Freshwater, the correct landing place, had been cleared. As a consequence, the Camerons, in the second wave of landings, also disembarked on the wrong beach taking a visual lead from the vessels and troops ahead of them. The tanks, while on the correct beaches, landed out of sequence and so, from the outset, the timing and coordination of the operation was jeopardised.

Although the participants 'thought on their feet', and salvaged many areas of the exercise, overall it was deemed a 'dismal failure' and as a consequence, the Dieppe raid was postponed.

However, lessons were learnt from this first exercise and changes were agreed and implemented and a second rehearsal, Yukon 2, took place on June 23rd with a much more successful outcome.

From early morning, Lyme Bay was filled with more than 80 vessels as they landed troops and then waited off shore for their withdrawal. Geoff Ackerman was a schoolboy in 1942 and recalls seeing the water off West Bay, filled with craft as he went to school, but when he returned to his hilltop vantage point at the end of the school day, they were gone.

The Churchill tanks which were being 'tested' in this exercise, proved very successful and made short work of the tubular metal tank defences on the beaches and negotiated the shingle beaches without problem. However, the ditches in Bothenhampton took their toll! Peter Williams, a long time resident of the village, watched the tanks crossing the fields near his home as they made their way towards Bridport and Bradpole. On his return from school later in the day, he discovered that not all had made it… the narrow lanes near the church had resulted in one tank sliding into a ditch and he watched its recovery.

Many residents of West Bay were moved out of the harbour area into rest centres in Bridport for the duration of the exercises, so did not witness events on the beach. However, some local people did come into contact with the troops, albeit briefly, as they made their way inland towards their targets. Barbara Bishop was living at Wanderwell at the time and was woken at dawn, by the sight and sound of 'foreign' troops. In the ensuing confusion the family did not recognise that the troops were French Canadians, and thought the threatened invasion by the Germans had started. When Barbara's father realised that it was French, not German that was being spoken, he reassured her from downstairs "It's not the enemy!"

Norah Warren, thought that she too had been caught up in the 'Invasion'. She was newly married, living in a bungalow just below Eype church and remembers being woken, very early in the morning. When she looked out of the window she saw soldiers with rifles all around the house, crouching down, and then moving across the grass. She soon discovered that they were Canadian and her overriding memory was of the youth of the soldiers who sat for a short time in her kitchen. She didn't know their regiment, but it may well have been Toronto's Royal Regiment of Canada, who had successfully landed on Blue beach (Eypesmouth) this time. She often wondered what had happened to them…

My father, Terry Meaney, could have told her.

He was one of the Royal Naval Commandos who landed with the Royal Regiment at Eypesmouth on June 23rd and was with them again at Puits on August 19 the day of the Combined Operations raid on Dieppe. The figures for Blue beach are stark enough. At Puits, of the 554 Canadians landed, 524 were killed, wounded or taken prisoner. My father, also lying wounded, saw only six men walk from the beach.

His quiet comment on an operation that ranks among the worst tragedies of the Second World War, came with typical understatement: *"At Eype, it went quite well, but when we got to the other side, it wasn't quite the same."*

American Soldiers in Bridport

by Robin Pearce

On Friday, November 5, 1943 members of the 1st Infantry Division arrived in the port of Liverpool. The next day they travelled by train to Dorchester and from there, by truck, to various parts of Dorset. One of the first to arrive was the 1st Reconnaissance Troop at 0130 on Wardon Hill, Sydling St. Nicholas. About the same time, the 5th Field Artillery Battalion reached Piddlehinton Camp. From then on, seemingly endless convoys of heavy trucks moved across Dorset and the 2nd Battalion of the 16th Infantry Regiment reached Bridport on the Saturday evening.

The Headquarters of the 16th Infantry Regiment was at Parnham House, Beaminster and the 2nd Battalion was one of three infantry battalions in the regiment. It was divided into four companies: E, F, G and H. Company H was based in the St. Andrew's Road area; Companies E and G were based at Walditch; Company F was at West Bay. The 2nd Battalion CO was Lieutenant Colonel Herbert C. Hicks, Jr. and his Command Post was in Downe Hall, Bridport.

Carl Monday (centre front) in Bridport with others from Headquarters Company platoon shortly after arriving from Sicily.
© Private Collection

The regiment's Service Company was also based in Bridport as well as the Battalion Medical Section. As D-Day approached, the 893rd Tank Destroyer Battalion moved to the town. Equipped with the formidable M-18 Tank Destroyer, it had its HQ and HQ Company as well as Companies A, B and C and a Medical Detachment. This unit went over to France after D-Day.

A total of around 2,000 men and women nursing officers gave the impression that the town was almost full of young GIs. With a civilian population of about 6,000, minus all the men and women who were in the British Armed Services, about one in every three people in Bridport was a young American soldier. They were exciting times for the town's inhabitants.

The infantrymen were of two kinds: those who had been fighting in North Africa and Sicily for over a year and those who had come over from America recently as replacements or reinforcements. Some of the battle-hardened troops were ill with malaria and other diseases, but they still joined the newcomers in a vigorous training programme. In February, 1944 they went to the American Amphibious Training Centre at Braunton, near Barnstaple. The centre had British and Canadian commandos among the training staff and all the GIs found it exceedingly tough. In March they took part in more amphibious landings on Slapton Sands, Devon in *Exercise Fox*. In May they returned for further amphibious landings in *Exercise Fabius*. Each of these exercises was made as close to the real thing as possible. They started off in Weymouth and Portland harbours and used the same landing craft and assault ships that would be used on D-day. *Exercise Tiger*, which involved the 4th Infantry Division training for the amphibious assault on Utah beach, was a disaster because German boats sank two Landing Ship Tanks (LSTs) just over 20 miles south of Stonebarrow Hill, near Charmouth. A total of 749 American soldiers were killed. Some of their bodies were washed up on the beaches of Lyme Bay. It was an event that was kept secret for many years.

Many buildings in the Bridport area were taken over by the Americans. These included fine houses like The Hyde at Walditch (Company G Command Post [CP] and officers' quarters), Downe Hall (Officers and Nursing Officers), Allington Court (Mess hall for Medical Section), cottages and bungalows at West Bay (Accommodation for Company F officers and enlisted men), The Masonic Hall (Billet for HQ Company men), The Literary and Scientific Institute (American Red Cross Club, Concert Hall for the 1st Infantry Division Orchestra and Medical Aid Station) and South Mill (Billet for men of the Personnel Section).

There were many Nissen and Quonset huts constructed, near the old Artillery and Infantry Drill Halls in Bridport. The Drill Halls were also used as billets. On the field behind the Real Tennis Court in Walditch there was a rectangular area marked out with white-painted stones for drill formations. Around this area were about half a dozen Quonset huts for enlisted men. NCOs were accommodated in the cottages opposite the tennis court building.

The troops were visited by other senior commanders. On January 16, 1944 General Montgomery also spoke to the American troops on Bridport Cricket Field. Officers of the regiment were addressed by General Omar Bradley in St. Mary's Church House on April 11. On this occasion General Bradley stayed at Parnham House.

Pubs and fish and chip shops were popular with the GIs. Some enterprising schoolboys set up fish and chip delivery services. Bill Payne, for instance, carried his orders in a pram and took them to the Personnel and Postal Sections in the cricket pavilion. Those billeted at the Masonic Hall enjoyed their breakfasts at cafés in East Street.

Dances were held in St. Mary's Church House in South Street and the same building was used for USO concerts. Jimmy Cagney went there with the show *Yankee Doodle Dandy* and a young lieutenant called John Mahan Brooks remembers having a drink with him after the show. The hall was also used for boxing classes and basketball games under the supervision of Lieutenant Anthony B. Zack, the Athletic and Recreation Officer. Boxer Carl R. Monday from St. Monroe in Michigan, a member of Headquarters Company won his Golden Gloves while he was in England. The 2nd Battalion Basketball Team also did well. They were the 1st Division champions and won 20 consecutive matches.

Another talented man in the 2nd Battalion was Corporal Sam Fuller of HQ Company who was billeted upstairs in St. Mary's Church House. After the war he became a film director and in *The Big Red One*, Lee Marvin took the part of a tough GI based on Sam Fuller.

By the beginning of May, the regiment was at its peak of preparedness and on May 17 billets and huts were "policed up", unwanted kit was packed into bags and foot lockers and convoys of trucks began to make their way to the marshalling areas. The 2nd Battalion was sent to Camp D-8, a woodland area in Winterborne Came parish, just

The 2nd Battalion Basketball Team won all 20 games in the 1943-1944 Season. They trained in St. Mary's Church House, South Street, Bridport. The sixth player is Carl Monday of Headquarters Company.
© Private Collection

across from the golf club. Altogether, 1494 troops with 143 vehicles were hidden in and around that small wood. The Battalion continued training until finally, on Wednesday, May 24, 1944 the camps were "sealed" and armed British troops patrolled the perimeter of the barbed wire fence. English money in units of ten shillings (50p) was collected in and the loose change was often thrown away. French currency was issued. Chemically impregnated clothing was given out and a new type of gas mask was also issued.

On May 31 they moved down to Weymouth harbour to embark on landing craft which took them out to the assault ship USS Henrico. The start of the greatest amphibious assault in history was about to take place. The 2nd Battalion was to land on Omaha Beach at H-Hour (0630) alongside the 3rd Battalion. Company E was on the section of beach known as *Easy Red*; on its left was Company F. The 3rd Battalion was to the left of the 2nd Battalion and landed on *Fox Green*. With alarming losses, the 2nd Battalion showed much bravery. Captain Joseph T. Dawson, CO of Company G from Walditch, for example, was awarded the Distinguished Service Cross for his brave action on the beach.

The 16th Infantry Regiment of the 1st Infantry Division fought alongside the 116th Infantry Regiment of the 29th Infantry Division. The latter was a National Guard Regiment and it was brought up from the Plymouth area to take part in the invasion.

Below are details from the provisional official Casualty Report for Companies E and F of the 2nd Battalion from Bridport on June 6-8, 1944, (D-Day and D+1):

Company E		
[Opening Strength – 8 officers and 211 enlisted men]	Officers	Men
Killed in Action	1	6
Missing in Action (believed killed)	1	0
Wounded in Action (evacuated)	1	78
TOTAL	**3**	**84**
Company F		
[Opening Strength – 9 officers and 218 enlisted men]		
Killed in Action	1	6
Missing in Action (believed killed)	4	0
Wounded in Action (evacuated)	2	64
TOTAL	**7**	**70**

These figures are taken from an official document which was compiled on Omaha Beach. The lists do not included the MIA (Missing in Action) "Stragglers", that is, those men who were separated from their unit because their landing craft had sunk, or because they landed on the wrong part of the beach. Many of them were killed or wounded. Some of the WIA (Wounded in Action) troops also died later in hospital. The provisional figures were bad enough, but when accurate figures were obtained, they were very bad for Companies E and F in particular.

As Colonel Gerald K. Griffin, Trustee of the 16th Infantry Regiment Association often says: "Freedom is never free." The 2nd Infantry Battalion, many of whom had been "adopted" by Bridport families or married Bridport girls, departed as quickly as it had arrived seven months before. Within a very short time, some of its members had made the ultimate sacrifice.

Sergeant Raymond Mohrlang in England, 1944

compiled by Chris Pamplin

This is a wonderful story; I made contact with Gary Mohrlang through eBay. I was buying a USAAF patch for my personal collection. He noticed we live at Bridport in England and wrote to tell me his father was stationed at Bridport awaiting embarkation to the D-Day landing beaches 60 years ago. These pictures were taken in England, before he joined his comrades in the big push across the Channel. I told Gary that Bridport Museum was holding an exhibition of official photographs, taken locally, of GI's in the war getting to know us Limeys (*US Troops in an English Village* was held in the Museum during 2004). These photographs are Sergeant Raymond Mohrlang's personal memory of his comrades in arms, and his band of brothers. The photos speak for themselves, a company of young men who have already been tested by battle, wait for the big push into Europe. They know what lies before them and they will show incredible bravery against all the odds. Here I let Gary take over the story of how his father, one of many soldiers, came to our aid 60 years ago.

Gary writes, "Until my dad's dying day, I don't believe I ever heard him refer to the

English as English, British, Brits or any other name you all may go by. It was always "Those Limeys" or "That Limey," but always with true admiration in his voice. He would tell us as children "When I was over there, those Limeys would have their bagpipers play right up front into battle!" "Can you imagine how brave those Limeys were!" or "Those Limeys knew how to do it right!" or "The Limeys have the right idea," etc. We always knew to whom he was referring.

The photos show my father Sergeant Raymond Mohrlang in England, May 1944, right before the Cross-Channel Attack.

He served in Capt. Joseph Dawson's Company G, 2nd Battalion, 16th Infantry Regiment, 1st Infantry Division. They were credited with being the first onto the bluffs overlooking Omaha Beach on June 6th, which he never talked about.

I learned about this through reading about the invasion and talking with some of his buddies. I am very proud of my father's war service.

His decorations and awards include the Combat Infantryman's Badge, Presidential Unit Citation with Oak Leaf Cluster, Silver Star Medal, Bronze Star Medal with Oak Leaf Cluster, Purple Heart Medal, Good Conduct Medal, Meritorious Unit Citation, EAME Campaign Medal with 6 Campaign Stars and Arrowhead Device (for Invasion Assaults on North Africa, Sicily and Normandy), the W.W.II Victory Medal and the French Foureguerre.

He was serving with Company G as a Staff Sergeant/Platoon Guide, when on November 20, 1944, he was severely wounded in the Huertgen Forest Battle, shortly after crossing the Siegfried Line in Germany. He was evacuated through England back to America and spent the next 4 years at Fitzsimmons General Hospital in Denver, Colorado. His wounds caught up with him and he passed away on Feb. 28, 1986. He is missed!"

Photographs taken by Sergeant Raymond Mohrlang, 1944

Photographs taken by Sergeant Raymond Mohrlang, 1944

The Big Red One in Bridport

by Celia Martin

Joseph Parke, who was born in Ireland in 1922, travelled with his family, to live in America when he was five years old. He joined the army in New York as soon as he could. By the time he arrived in Bridport he was Private First Class Joseph P. Parke No. 12022214 in the 16th Infantry of the First United States Army, now often referred to as The Big Red One.

He was stationed in Bridport and was billeted in the building in North Street, which is now the Conservative Club. Coincidentally his brother Jim Parke was billeted at Abbotsbury. The 16th Infantry were in Dorset while preparing for the Normandy invasion and Joseph was lucky enough to meet an Irish girl called Mary Conlon whose family had come to Bridport to work at Pymore Mill in 1939. Mary and Joseph were married at the Catholic Church in Bridport in 1944.

Joseph Parke, circa 1943
© Private Collection

It is also the story of a young man of extreme bravery who went over the Channel to fight the Nazis on D-Day and survived. He was awarded the Distinguished Service Cross for staying behind to defuse the situation while the rest of Company 'H' moved out to attack from another direction. In the four hours that he was on his own he disorganised the enemy with a continuous and accurate hail of fire while over three hundred artillery shells were fired towards his position.

After the War Joseph Parke joined the American Air Force and returned to Britain, this time with his wife Mary and their first child, Jo, who was born at Pymore. Joseph died in the 1970s but his wife Mary and seven children all live in the United States.

Mary Parke with Family in 2002.
© Private Collection

The 16th General Hospital, Bridport

by Celia Martin

When Muriel Engelman heard that Bridport was preparing to celebrate the 60th anniversary of D-Day she contacted the West Dorset Research Centre and sent some photographs that she had taken in 1944 when she was an American nurse with the 16th General Hospital. They had been operating a hospital in North Wales until just after D-Day when at short notice they were moved to Bridport where they spent the month of July billeted at Downe Hall preparing to sail for France.

Muriel describes that day. "We travelled all night and arrived in Bridport, at about 8.a.m, tired and hungry, and with no place to go because no one expected us. They finally herded us together and marched us to Downe Hall which was stripped of everything except cockroaches and rats that roamed the place freely."

The photographs show their life in the garden at Downe Hall and

Wedding Reception at Downe Hall,
July 1944
© Private Collection

Nurses on the beach at West Bay,
July 1944
© Private Collection

the male medical and dental officers who lived nearby at Mountfield. She says that the month of July was the hottest on record and they were allowed to go to the beach at West Bay to swim which "was a wonderful respite from hospital routine and we were all tanned and healthy looking by the time we left England."

On the way to the beach they were befriended by Mr and Mrs S. R. Edwards who lived at Jessomene (now known as Eypeleaze) on the West Bay Road where they were invited to have hot baths in a real bath tub whenever they liked, a luxury they had missed since leaving the States.

The highlight of the month was when one of the nurses married an American Air Force Lieutenant in Bridport and they held the reception afterwards at Downe Hall. The nurses gathered at the front entrance waiting to catch the bride's bouquet. Another member of the team later married Raymond Baxter, before he became the well known BBC broadcaster. They came back to visit Downe Hall about fifteen years ago and were delighted to be invited in for tea.

The 16th General Hospital finally left Bridport and sailed to Normandy where they stayed for seven weeks and then spent the rest of the war operating a 1000 bed tent hospital at Liege in Belgium till well after VE Day.

And because of this event Muriel Engelman and the Edwards grandchildren have made contact again after sixty years.

Edwards Grandchildren, 1944
© Private Collection

American Murder at Lyme Regis

by Nigel Clarke

Nestling in a valley along the Dorset and Devon border is the ancient town of Lyme Regis. A small coastal fishing community, which prior to WW2 was an isolated backwater that came alive for the brief pre-war summer tourist trade. Many of the inhabitants were locally born and few travelled far or left the area. The population in 1943 was about 2704 slightly swelled by evacuees escaping the bombing in the cities. By 1944, one in five residents of the town was an American serviceman.

When WW2 started many of the local men were drafted into the services and were away from the area for over four years. Only a few young men were left in the town. Rationing was soon introduced and the beach and harbour was closed to civilians. The fishing boats were pushed up onto the beach and the Cobb was mined. Dorset awaited the expected German invasion.

Lyme Regis was parochial and until the War little had disrupted the local cycle of life. The last event to place Lyme Regis on the historical stage was in 1685 when the Duke of Monmouth (the illegitimate son of Charles II), raised a rebellion against the Crown, and landed on the beach with his supporters.

In 1943 a battalion of Black American servicemen arrive in Lyme Regis. They were part of an advance team sent to prepare camps and facilities for the 1st Battalion of the US 16th Infantry Regiment. The entire regiment was to be located in West Dorset prior to the D-Day Landings. All over Dorset and Devon, vast numbers of American troops were billeted and camped around the towns, villages and fields of the counties. Dorset and Devon came under the military control of the United States Army.

Lyme Regis changed overnight. Strangers in a small town are always exotic. Black faces were rare and the black soldiers were new, exciting and wealthy (the average pay of the GI during WW2 was three times that of the local rate). The new arrivals soon settled and mixed freely with the local population. The black soldiers had the novel experience of dating white girls. There were no black girls in Lyme Regis. It is reported that a brothel was established in a house on Cobb Road.

For a few months the black GI's were the only American servicemen in Lyme Regis but in November 1943 a second group of American soldiers arrived in Lyme Regis. The 16th Infantry Regiment of the 1st Infantry Division. The division had fought through North Africa and Italy. Many of the soldiers were battle hardened and emotionally scarred from the war.

Lyme Regis was their first break from the battlefront after many months of fighting. The new arrivals were allocated bunkhouses on the eastern edge of the town while their officers moved into Kent House, St Michael's and took over other large guesthouses and hotels in the resort.

The American troops were a novelty and an attraction to the local population. The American friendliness was in contrast to the normal English reserve. Local girls were invited to American camp dances. The Americans were not restricted to the normal war rations of the English civilians. Chocolate, turkey, cigarettes, cakes and large quantities of other foods were available. The Americans were also able to obtain make-up and nylon stockings, which had disappeared from the British market in 1939.

Black GIs in Dorchester, during World War 2
© Private Collection

The Americans introduced new music, totally different from the staid "English Tea Dance", the Jitterbug and Swing encouraging contact between the sexes.

Churchill's government had discussed concerns about the stationing of black American troops in the United Kingdom. The American Army policy during the World War Two was to segregate black servicemen from other races. Black soldiers were normally not allowed to fight as front line troops and performed mostly service and support duties. Black and white US Soldiers did not meet socially and many of the recreational facilities were separate and segregated, such as the cinema, dances, pubs and canteens.

Each group would have their own camp, sleeping and dining facilities. Separate arrangements were made for both groups. Although both served in the US army segregation was the established practice of the period. There was little mixing between the races and on occasion tension spilled over into fighting between the two groups.

At Maiden Newton and Evershot fighting and clashes took place between the black and white GI's. In Yeovil the local cinema was divided up, into separate black and white seating areas. Joe Louis, the heavy weight boxing champion, sat in the white section by accident and was briskly told to move.

The tension between the two groups of soldiers at Lyme Regis was soon evident and came to ahead one morning in late May 1944. A minor argument erupted at the "PX Store" the American equivalent of the NAAFI, between black and white American soldiers. The store was located in the Marine Theatre, off Church Street.

A black soldier wanted to purchase a "Zipper Lighter" although the supply was restricted to white soldiers only. A fierce argument occurred and continued out onto main road near the Town Hall and Rock Point, towards the bottom of the town. The row soon deteriorated into a fight during the fracas a bayonet was produced and used by one of the white soldiers to kill a black American GI, who was fatally stabbed through the heart.

News of the murder quickly spread through the town and separate groups of both black and white soldiers rushed back to their camps to obtain weapons. The resident American Military Police were outnumbered and could do little to control the escalating violence.

The violence at Lyme Regis was in danger of spiralling out of control. The two groups rushed back into town and met in the narrow road outside the medieval guildhall, in the centre of town. The soldiers were armed with clubs, rifles and machine guns. Shortly before the trouble started two local policemen arrived on the scene. Although unarmed and outnumbered they were able to diffuse the situation and both groups returned to their respective camps.

The incident described above took place and remains in the folklore of the town of Lyme Regis, and is remembered by a dwindling band or residents and has been corroborated by them.

During the course of my research I can find no evidence that anyone was ever charged with this murder or found any official papers dealing with this case. The murder was not reported in the local newspapers, which were censored during the war. The police have destroyed their records for this period of the town's history.

On the 6th June at 06:43, units of the 1st Division who had been stationed at Lyme Regis were among the first units to land onto Omaha beach, in Normandy. They suffered numerous casualties over 1638 men were killed or wounded.

The black service corps left Lyme Regis shortly afterwards following the frontline troops through France, although their history is less well documented. The story and friendships established with these black troops is now a dying memory.

US 66th Infantry Division – Not forgotten after 60 years

by Jane Ferentzi-Sheppard

In late November 1944, part of the US 66th Infantry Division arrived in Dorset. The Division included the 262, 263 & 264 Infantry Regiments, with reconnaissance, medical, artillery, special troops and a band. By the 12th December, the total number of US 66th Infantry Division had reached 5,500. The men were stationed all over West Dorset, including Piddlehinton Camp, Marabout Barracks, Maumbury Rings and Poundbury in Dorchester, Bridport and Lyme

Members of Company B 262 Infantry, enjoying free time in Nantes, April 1945
© Private Collection

Regis. They spent their time training in the Dorset countryside preparing to cross over to France and join the Allied push into Germany.

They were nicknamed the Black Panther Division because of their very distinctive shoulder patch. The Division was activated in July of 1943 and had extensive training in the US before arriving in Europe. The Division was always losing men to be back up troops in Europe. Many of the men who came to Dorset were 18 – 21 year olds who had only recently joined the army.

There were opportunities to meet the local girls, as this invitation to a party below suggests. The young men threw themselves into a social life in rural Dorset. On December 8th, Company I, 262 Infantry held a 'Hello England' party. The notice read:

The boys of Company I are at it again.
They're reeling and rocking and filled with vim.
They're giving a party to celebrate,
And would like to have you for a date.
So put on your party clothes, and come on down.
And we'll show you how to go to town.

Everyone was getting ready to celebrate Christmas in Dorset. Unfortunately the events in the Ardennes on the 16th December meant the 'Battle of the Bulge' had begun and the Division's time in England was drawing to a close. At Piddlehinton many small parties had been arranged for the evening of 23rd December, to which local girls had been invited.

There was to be a good supply of beer and dance music. A Christmas tree had transformed the mess hall and the cooks had begun roasting the turkeys when the order to pull out arrived.

John Koch 18, Company D, 262 Infantry Regiment, from Indiana, remembers the three weeks of training in the beautiful rolling fields around Dorchester. He was on guard duty at the Keep, Marabout Barracks, on the morning of 23rd December 1944 when they were put on alert and told they were to be shipped out. At noon the order came for them to be ready to move out by 6.00 p.m. that evening. Trains were waiting in Dorchester to take the troops to Southampton. By 2.00 a.m. on Sunday 24th December John Koch was standing on the pier at Southampton. Two ships were waiting the SS Leopoldville and HMS Cheshire for the troops to board. By sheer chance John and his group who had been standing round singing Christmas Carols, chose the nearer ship the Cheshire. Little did they know this choice would change their lives forever.

SS Leopoldville.
© Private collection

There had been confusion in the loading of the men and when they arrived in Southampton some were separated from their squads and companies. Men from the 264 and 262 Regiments except Companies A, B, C & D of the 262, were on the Leopoldville, the 263 Regiment and the rest of the 262 were placed on the Cheshire. The ships were filled to capacity with about 2,500 troops each aboard. They were joined on the crossing by a small convoy of British ships which included HMS Brilliant.

The sea was rough and the crossing long. Suddenly about five miles out of Cherbourg tragedy struck. The Leopoldville was hit by a torpedo from a German U-boat. There was a delay in getting rescue ships there and the ship sank with the loss of 763 GIs, some 493 bodies were never found. The destroyer HMS Brilliant came alongside, Bob Clothier from Maiden Newton, remembers how difficult it was. Ropes were thrown at the Leopoldville and we encouraged the men to jump. We rescued as many as we could but the sea was very rough and the two ships kept banging against each other, but we took about 750 survivors.

The story of the Leopoldville disaster remained untold for nearly fifty years. Families had no idea what had happened to their loved ones. Information remained classified and has slowly come to light.

After the disaster, the Division was no longer a full combat unit so they were sent to relieve the 94th Division in the St. Nazaire and Lorient areas of Brittany instead of to the Ardennes. Some 28,000 Germans were defending their submarine bases and pens. The Division was involved in frequent ambush patrols to take prisoners; and reconnaissance patrols to learn about gun positions. Fierce fighting took place until the official surrender on the 10 May 1945. The Division was then moved to Germany on occupation duty, then to Marseille and sailed home on 27th October 1945. The total casualties for the 66th Division were 1,947 and 268 wounded.

Jane Ferentzi-Sheppard planting a tree in remembrance of the GIs who lost their lives on 24 December 1944.
© Roger Guttridge

On December 23rd 2004, sixty years to the day that the troops left, 800 trees were planted at Piddlehinton Camp, now an Enterprise Park, in memory of those young GIs who lost their lives on Christmas Eve 1944. Bob Clothier (HMS Brilliant) was a guest and planted one of the trees. I planted a tree on behalf of the 'Panther Veterans Organisation' and the American Embassy was represented by Lt Col Rich Gibbons who expressed gratitude on behalf of the US government for what had been done in memory of the American soldiers. The beech trees will be a permanent memorial to those 'boys' who visited our beloved county of Dorset for five short weeks in 1944.

This article is dedicated to the men of Co B, 262nd Infantry Regiment and John Koch, Co D, 262 who all boarded the Cheshire that night and which changed their lives for ever and to those 763 GIs who lost their lives on the Leopoldville.

⚭

Further reading:

S.S. Leopoldville Disaster December 24, 1944, Allan Andrade

Leopoldville Troopship Disaster, Allan Andrade

Hitler's U-Boat Fortresses, Randolph Bradham, Co E, 262nd Regiment

Bridport after World War 2 (1945-1953)

by Paul Willis

When the Japanese Government signed the surrender agreement, which officially ended the Second World War on 2 September 1945, it was estimated that over 52,000,000[1] people had died during the six year conflict. Although figures vary, approximately 357,000 British citizens died by the conflict's end. In addition 326,000 and 46,000 British citizens were injured and recorded as missing respectively.[2]

Although these statistics provide an indication of the devastation of the Second World War, they do not provide the stories of those who suffered and died, or those who endured and survived. Everyone living in Britain at that time was personally touched by the War in one way or another.

The parade of service companies and local organisations to mark V.E. Day, May 1945.
© Photograph by courtesy of the Bridport Museum Trust

Even though the War resulted in many hardships, it also led to many positive changes in British society. The country experienced a powerful sense of unity. There was a general belief that after the War Britain would be a better place with full employment, a universal education system, social welfare, a national health service, and redesigned and modernised towns and cities; all the social amenities that had been lacking for the majority of people before the War. The general feeling after the War was that Churchill's Tory

Government would not deliver the improvements in social services that the population desired.

On 5th July 1945 Clement Attlee's Labour Party was elected to power with a huge majority. Under the Attlee Government Britain experienced some of the country's greatest changes; nothing less than a reconstruction of the nation. A programme of Nationalisation began with the Bank of England (1946), Coal Industry, Cable and Wireless (1947), Railways, Electricity, Gas, and National Health Insurance (1948) and Iron and Steel (1951).

In spite of the reforming enthusiasm and experience of many members of Attlee's cabinet, Post World War II Britain, was still an era of austerity, as the devastating economic impact of the War became evident.

Severe economic measures were imposed to meet the enormous war debt. These measures caused hardships that were only made worse in 1947 by one of the worst winters on record. A fuel shortage severely curtailed exports, food was still rationed, and in 1948 even bread and potatoes were rationed (both had been exempt during the War). For the most part, rationing continued until 1949, with the availability of some items remaining controlled until 1954.

Victory Party, Bothenhampton, 6 October 1946. About 150 people gathered together in the centre of the village to celebrate the end of the Second World War.
© Photograph by courtesy of the Bridport Museum Trust

The end of the Second World War brought the community of Bridport out onto the streets to celebrate. The Town rejoiced in style with both civic events and street parties. The people of Bridport had many reasons to be proud of their wartime efforts with raising money and supplying the country with wartime equipment. Over the next 8 years life returned to a new routine with the revival of many organisations and events.

The first Welcome Home Fund distribution of wallets containing £5 and Treasury notecases to all demobilised men and women took place at the Drill Hall on 15 February 1946. However some felt this was not enough. It was suggested that the Borough Council should provide "a decent job with decent pay and a decent house (and) security from want"[3] for the Town's service personnel.

Many town improvements had been set aside since 1939. The Bridport Borough Council was under pressure to implement measures that addressed the needs of the community, such as, new housing, a new school, and other public services. The Council received much criticism from the County Council and the wider community for the lack of pace in building much needed housing. 218 houses were built from 1945 to 1952. Some families were however unable to pay rent of 39s. 9d. per week and by the end of 1953 155 people were still on the waiting list for a new house.

The supply of water was another major concern for many years immediately after the War. It was a regular occurrence for many households to experience water and electricity cuts. There were heavy fines for people using water or electricity illegally. Some people reverted to collecting water from wells and roadside ditches which were usually not fit for consumption.

Bridport did not suffer the same severity of food rationing as some towns, however gift parcels from across the Empire were regularly distributed to the needy. Some inventive methods were devised to beat the ration. On Saturday 13 August 1949 Cornick's Store in West Street, sold over 2¾ tons of sweets to the public before sweets were placed back on the ration. Mr Percy Woodhall, the proprietor of the White Lion Hotel at Broadwindsor served badger sandwiches as "the best way of helping out the 8d meat ration."[4]

The Post War years were also a time of change for the Town's staple rope and net making industries. Edwards and Son Ltd. and Rendell and Coombs amalgamated in late July 1945. Two major fires caused great destruction – the first in a warehouse in Magdalen Lane owned by Messrs James and Co. and the other at the Messrs Joseph Gundry and Co. Ltd site. However the major change to affect the industry was the revolution from natural to synthetic fibres. Mr C.W. Edwards stated, "There can be no doubt that such fibres will replace natural ones…we are constantly engaged in experiment and adaptation of the plant so as to be fully abreast of the latest developments…"[5]

Bridport, like the rest of the country, was looking forward to the future. During 1948, the Bridport Chamber of Commerce held the "Bridport 1948 Exhibition" at the Artillery Drill Hall. The trade exhibition displayed the labour-saving devices, new fashions, and latest designs from the town's traders. The exhibition was "a fine example of the harmony and enterprising spirit of Bridport's tradesmen."[6] At the end of January 1952 many of the townsfolk saw themselves on the screen at the Bridport Palace Cinema when a film based on the town and its rope and net industry was shown for the first time. The film one of the *Come With Me* series was made by the National Screen Services with the cooperation of Bridport Industries Ltd.

In June 1953 it was hoped that the Charter Pageant festivities would herald a new age of prosperity for the town and its people. The future did look promising for Bridport with the restrictions of rationing coming to an end, new homes being constructed, and a number of internationally important industries generating income and employment in the town. However the Town would need to face new challenges in the future from changes in old work practices, a changing modern culture, and a new demand for consumer goods and prosperity.

Bridport Royal Charter Pageant, 24 June 1953
© Photograph by courtesy of the Bridport Museum Trust

Footnotes

1 Figure taken from The History Place web-site:
   http://www.historyplace.com/worldwar2/timeline/statistics.htm

2 Figures take from The World at War. History of World War 2 1939-1945. A Military Historical Website.
   http://www.euronet.nl/users/wilfried/ww2/epilogue.htm

3 Bridport News Friday May 4 1945, Letter to the Editor from TC Johnson, Bedford Place, Bridport.

4 Bridport News Friday February 16 1951, Mr Percy Woodhall, White Lion Hotel, Broadwindsor.

5 Bridport News Friday December 18 1953 Bridport Industries maintain 20% on ordinary shares.

6 Bridport News Friday September 24 1948.

Contributors

Nigel J. Clarke runs a publishing company in Lyme Regis. Books include *Adolf Hitler's Holiday Snaps, Smuggler's Tales of Dorset and Devon*. For more information check Nigel's website: www.njcpublications.demon.co.uk/index.html

Michael Corgan was born in Hampstead in 1933. Evacuated to Northampton during the War he went on to Willesden County Grammar School before serving in the Middle East, in the RAF, spending some time at Ismailia with the Royal Engineer Inland Water Transport Squadron. After a career in retail management he moved into window display graduating to forming his own company supplying services to exhibitors at trade shows, from the smallest requirement up to the design and construction of large and complex stands. On retirement he studied History, completing his BA at St. Mary's, Strawberry Hill, and latterly his MA, at Exeter. His MA dissertation was on the impact of the Second World War on the Bridport area.

Jane Ferentzi-Sheppard was born in 1945 and went to Colyton Grammar School. After training as a history teacher she spent 22 years in Germany teaching and training teachers to teach English. Since her retirement she has gained an MA in Local & Regional History and now lectures on local, family and migration history all over the country. One of her special interests is the Americans in Dorset during World War II.

Elizabeth Gale (née Buckler) was born in Burton Bradstock, where her paternal family can be traced back to 1610. Her maternal family are known to have lived in Dorset since 1700. She attended Bridport Grammar School and the Dorset College of Agriculture. Throughout her life she has been involved with many local organisations and is the founder member of several, including the West Dorset Family History Group and Brit Valley Rotary Club. Now retired, she concentrates on local history and is following up her previous book, *Farmers, Fishermen and Flax Spinners*, with an account of the sale of the Pitt-Rivers Estate, in West Dorset.

Rene Gerryts reporter for the Bridport and Lyme Regis News.

Valerie Jeanes (née Stoodley) was born in Bridport and was educated at St Mary's Church School and Bridport Grammar School. After leaving school she worked in the offices of Joseph Gundry & Co. In 1962, Valerie moved with her husband and three children to Bristol. She returned to Bridport in 1991. Her paper in this publication has been taken from interviews with local residents recorded during 1984. She is currently compiling a Memorial Book of local servicemen and civilian casualties of the Second World War.

Celia Martin MA in Local and Regional studies. Researcher in local history, author of *The Bridport Trade* (2003).

Sheila Meaney born in Bristol, one of the baby-boom generation. Sheila moved to Bridport in 1988 with her family and worked at St. Mary's Primary School. Since her retirement as Head-teacher, Sheila has followed her interest in family and local history. She has also been involved with many children's charities and is currently studying and crying over a Master of Arts in Irish Studies.

Chris Pamplin and his wife Fiona are dancers; jive & jitterbug is their thing and this has lead to an interest in the American GIs of the Second World War. They currently live in Weymouth, with their four month old daughter Grace who shows promising signs of dancing! Weymouth is one of the ports where the GIs set sail for the Normandy Beaches Chris is a member of the Military Vehicle Trust. His real job is as a geologist working on the Jurassic Coast. Find out more at www.gijive.co.uk

Robin Pearce was born at Hoyland in Yorkshire in 1934. He was educated at Wintringham Grammar School, Grimsby. From 1953-1955 he served in the Royal Navy as a Leading Coder (Special). For thirty-five years he taught in a number of secondary schools. Since retirement he has researched military history and has published *Operation Wasservogel* (1996), *Dorset Attacked Dorset Defended* (1999) and *Seven Months to D-Day: An American Regiment in Dorset* (2000),

Bob Pearson a retired freelance journalist with a particular interest in natural history, was born in Carshalton, Surrey, in 1938. He is a qualified table tennis coach and teaches the sport voluntarily at Beaminster School. Soon after moving to Beaminster with his wife Margaret in 1999, he started a quarterly magazine called Around & About Beaminster for the local civic society. He writes and edits articles dealing with all aspects of the town's life, past and present.

Holly Robinson was born in Wokingham, Berkshire in 1976, moving to Wiltshire at the age of nine. She was educated at Hardenhuish School in Chippenham before going on to read law at University College London. On the completion of her degree she returned to Wiltshire and in 1998 landed a job as a trainee reporter on one of her local newspapers, *The Wiltshire Times* and *Chippenham News*. She qualified as a senior reporter in September 2000, and during six years at the paper worked her way up to news editor. In August 2004 she moved to Dorset to become editor of the *Bridport and Lyme Regis News*.

Fiona Taplin was born in the North-East of England and gained a Degree in English at Durham University. She started her teaching career at Tynemouth High School in 1962, and came to Bridport in 1966 to teach English at Colfox School. After a short break in the early seventies, she taught at the school from 1974 until retirement in 2001. She has written several articles, including one on the Colfox family for *Dorset Life* magazine. She is currently completing a history of schools in Bridport from 1238 to 2000, entitled "This Good Work", to be published later this year.

Janet Tilley (née Boon) was born in Dorchester in 1934 to a family involved in the business life of West Dorset. An only child, she completed her education at the Dorchester County School for Girls. At the age of 18, a keen amateur soprano soloist, Janet won the Gold Medal of the Associated Board of the Royal Schools of Music. Janet gained the highest marks in Great Britain and Ireland for Grade VII Singing. She worked as a secretary for her father until her marriage in 1956. Janet has been involved in family research since 1975.

Paul Willis is currently the curator of the Bridport Museum. He has worked in both museums and art galleries in Australia and in the UK. At present he is working on a paper that investigates the relationship between photographic portraiture and the perception of the self.